DISCOVERY GUIDE

FAITH LESSONS™

walk

as jesus WALKED

The Faith Lessons™ Series with Ray Vander Laan

DISCOVERY GUIDE

FAITH LESSONS™

walk

as Jesus WALKED

MAKING DISCIPLES

FOCUS ON THE FAMILY®

Ray Vander Laan

with Stephen & Amanda Sorenson

ZONDERVAN®

ZONDERVAN.com/
AUTHORTRACKER
follow your favorite authors

Walk as Jesus Walked Small Group Edition Discovery Guide
Copyright © 2006 by Ray Vander Laan

Requests for information should be addressed to:

Zondervan, *Grand Rapids, Michigan 49530*

ISBN-10: 0-310-27117-7
ISBN-13: 978-0-310-27117-8

All photos courtesy of Ray Vander Laan

All maps courtesy of The Image Group

Interior design by Michelle Espinoza

Printed in the United States of America

08 09 10 11 12 • 18 17 16 15 14 13 12 11 10 9 8 7 6 5

contents

Introduction

Because God speaks to us through the Scriptures, studying them is a rewarding experience. The inspired human authors of the Bible, as well as those to whom the words were originally given, were primarily Jews living in the Near East. God's words and actions spoke to them with such power, clarity, and purpose that they wrote them down and carefully preserved them as an authoritative body of literature.

God's use of human servants in revealing himself resulted in writings that clearly bear the stamp of time and place. The message of the Scriptures is, of course, eternal and unchanging—but the circumstances and conditions of the people of the Bible are unique to their times. Consequently, we most clearly understand God's truth when we know the cultural context within which he spoke and acted, and the perception of the people with whom he communicated. This does not mean that God's revelation is unclear if we don't know the cultural context. Rather, by learning how to think and approach life as the people of the Bible did, modern Christians will deepen their appreciation and understanding of God's Word. To fully apply the message of the Bible, we must enter their world and familiarize ourselves with their culture.

That is the purpose of this study. The events and people of the Bible are presented in their original settings. Although the DVD segments offer the latest archaeological research, this series is not intended to be a definitive historical, cultural, or geographical study of the lands and times of the Bible. No original scientific discoveries are revealed here. My goal is simply to help us better understand God's revealed mission for our lives by enabling us to hear and see his words in their original context.

Go! And Make Disciples

The mission of God's people has always been to live *so that the world would know that their God was the true God.* This was true when the Hebrews left Egypt and possessed the Promised Land. This was true during the years of the exile in Babylon. It was true during the time Jesus lived on earth after the Jews had returned to Israel. And it was true for the disciples of Jesus who followed him as their Rabbi and, after his death and resurrection, obeyed his command to go out into the world and make disciples.

When Jesus came to earth to bring the good news of the kingdom of God and to offer himself as the perfect sacrifice to redeem the whole human race, he also chose disciples who would continue proclaiming his message and making disciples long after he returned to heaven. Jesus selected his disciples from a unique people in a unique place—a four-by-six-mile area on the northwestern shores of the Sea of Galilee. The Jews living in this part of Israel were the most obedient, faithful follow-ers of God to be found. These people knew the Scriptures, they knew how to apply the teaching of Scripture, and they were committed to obeying God in everything every day of their lives. From among them, Jesus chose a handful to carry the news of his kingdom to the world.

To some, Jesus' disciples would seem like an unlikely group. To their world, they weren't the brightest and the best Bible scholars; most of them were fishermen. They didn't know their way around the huge, sophisticated cities of the Roman Empire; they came from small, rural villages. But they had just what Jesus needed—the commitment, the passion, the desire to be his *talmidim*. For three and a half years, the disciples walked with Jesus. They followed him everywhere. They did everything they could to learn to be like Jesus—to know and interpret the Scriptures as he did, to pray as he did, to obey God's laws as he did, to love as he did, to proclaim the news of God's kingdom as he did, and to make disciples as he did.

Before he ascended to heaven, Jesus commanded them to go out into the world and make disciples. And they did. One of the places they went was Asia Minor—the most sophisticated, prosperous, immoral, per-verted, educated, and religious (but pagan) region in the whole Roman Empire! And when the disciples lived out the message of the kingdom of God and made disciples in Asia Minor, it impacted that region like an earthquake. In little more than a century, that region had become predominantly Christian.

In this study, we will investigate the world they went into and how the disciples made such a great impact. This is important to us because our world is much like the world of Asia Minor. If we expect to make the impact the disciples did, then we must learn to be like them—that is, like Jesus. The life of faith is not a vague, otherworldly experience. Rather, it is being faithful to God right now, in the place and time in which he has put us. God wants his people in the game, not on the bench. Our mission as Christians today is the same one God gave to the Israelites when they possessed the Promised Land, the same one Jesus gave to his disciples. We are to love the Lord our God with all our heart, with all our soul, and with all our might, and to love our neighbors as ourselves so that through us *the world may know that our God is the one true God.*

The assumptions of Biblical writers

Biblical writers assumed that their readers were familiar with Near Eastern geography, history, and culture. They used a language, which like all languages, is bound by culture and time. Therefore, understanding the Scriptures involves more than knowing what the words mean. We need to understand those words from the perspective of the people who used them.

Unfortunately, many Christians do not have even a basic knowledge of the world and people of the Bible. This series is designed to help solve that problem. We will be studying the people and events of the Bible in their geographical, historical, and cultural contexts. Once we know the *who*, *what*, and *where* of a Bible story, we will be able to better understand the *why*. By deepening our understanding of God's Word, we can strengthen our relationship with God.

The people whom God chose as his instruments—the people to whom he revealed himself—lived in the Near East where people typically described their world and themselves in concrete terms. Their language was one of pictures, metaphors, and examples rather than ideas, definitions, and abstractions. Whereas we might describe God as omniscient or onmipresent (knowing everything and present everywhere), they would have preferred to describe God by saying, "The Lord is my

Shepherd." Thus, the Bible is filled with concrete images: God is our Father, and we are his children. God is the Potter, and we are the clay. Jesus is the Lamb killed on Passover. The kingdom of heaven is like the yeast a woman took and mixed into flour. He will separate the people as a shepherd separates the sheep from the goats.

These people had an Eastern mind-set rather than a Western mind-set. Whereas Westerners tend to collect information to find the right answer, Hebrew thought stresses the process of discovery as well as the answer. So as you go through this study, use it as an opportunity to deepen your understanding of who God is and to grow in your relationship with him.

Run!:
The passion of Elijah

Each of us is passionate about something. Whether it's biking or golf, music or gardening, hunting or travel, photography or our grandchildren, we strive to devote as much time and energy to what fires up our passion as is appropriate ... and sometimes more than is appropriate. When we speak of the things we're passionate about, excitement dances across our faces and echoes in our voices.

But how many of us are truly passionate about our walk with Jesus? Although we may devote considerable time to worship, Bible study, prayer, and similar activities, is our daily walk with Jesus—how we live out our faith through personal discipleship—our deepest passion? Do we devote our best effort to our walk with Jesus? Does our relationship with him animate our conversations and energize our steps? Do other people notice our devotion, and does how we walk with Jesus inspire them to do the same?

For most of us, it's all too easy to have plenty of passion for some things but little zeal for our walk with Jesus. Our less-than-zealous obedience to God and his Word communicates that our spiritual walk is not something that excites us, and that influences how we live out our faith. We become complacent and apathetic about our relationship with God.

Yet God desires that his people live for him with passion. The religious Jews of Jesus' day understood intense devotion and zeal for God. They honored the passion and zeal of the ancient heroes of the faith—Moses, Phinehas, Hezekiah, Elijah, and so many more. They sought to emulate the fire these heroes showed in their walk with God, their devotion to Scripture, and their commitment to obedience. And they readily recognized those among them who lived with a passionate zeal for God.

Jesus the Messiah was not a laid-back, unemotional, matter-of-fact teacher. He lived with an intensity for God that few have ever known.

He clearly fulfilled the ancient prophecy: "zeal for your house consumes me" (Psalm 69:9). In fact, he displayed such great zeal for God that he was even mistaken for Elijah—the zealous Old Testament prophet who gave God everything he had. Jesus too gave everything, even his very life, in obedience to God.

Jesus challenges those who believe in him to become his disciples—his *talmidim*—to follow in his steps and become like him. So to be a disciple of Jesus is to walk zealously with God and make disciples as he did. The Jewish disciples of Jesus—including Peter, John, and Paul—understood this call for passionate discipleship. And they lived it. But Jesus sent his disciples out of the Jewish world and into a Hellenistic world that did not know Jesus and that had never heard of the passion of Elijah. It was a world not unlike the world into which he sends us today.

So in this session, amidst the spectacular ruins of the Roman city, Aphrodisias, we'll see how the disciples translated Jesus' call to passionate discipleship into the language and images the Roman culture already understood. We'll see how they used the people's knowledge of sports and the arena games to communicate the total dedication and intense passion needed to "run" the spiritual race in order to win. To give everything you have, your whole self, in order to win the prize is an image the Greek and Roman world understood. It is one our culture understands as well.

opening Thoughts (4 minutes)

The Very Words of God

> *I have been very zealous for the LORD God Almighty.*
>
> 1 Kings 19:14

Think About It

Close your eyes for a moment and imagine that you could see Jesus as he walked and taught in the villages of Galilee. How would you describe his appearance and demeanor—the way he sounded as he spoke, the look in his eyes, the way he moved as he walked? What do you think you would notice about him? Which heroes of the Bible, or our own time and culture, do you imagine as portraying some of the characteristics or qualities of Jesus?

DVD Notes (22 minutes)

The passion of Elijah

The passion of the Olympic games

Competing to honor the king

Surrounded by witnesses

DVD Highlights (4 minutes)

1. What did you learn about the prophet Elijah, Jesus, and the disciples that you had never before realized?

    In what ways do the images Ray Vander Laan presents of these men change your idea of what it means to walk as Jesus walked?

2. What was the point of the Olympic games played in stadiums, such as the one at Aphrodisias, throughout the Roman Empire?

    How does this knowledge help you to better understand what Paul intended to convey through references to athletic training and competition in his descriptions of what it means to walk as Jesus walked?

3. How often have you thought that the way you run your spiritual race today is a witness to those you leave behind? What does it take to run your spiritual race in such a way that you make a powerful statement of who God is and encourage others who see you to run well?

The hippodrome at Caesarea

small group Bible Discovery and Discussion (19 minutes)

The Zeal of Elijah

God loves his people with great passion and devotion and has always called those who say they love him to live for him with zeal—with a consuming passion to do his will and vigorously maintain his honor in all circumstances. That's what it means to "love the LORD your God with all your heart and with all your soul and with all your strength" (Deuteronomy 6:5). So whether they lived during Bible times or live today, godly people are consumed by an ardent zeal to be faithful to God's Word and exalt him in everything they do, say, and think. Their intensity is obvious to everyone they meet.

Elijah was a servant of God who is still remembered for his passionate devotion to God. Let's look at how Elijah walked with God during a key event in his life recorded in 1 Kings 18–19. His story will help us better understand the ancient Jewish desire to be zealous — totally devoted — to God.

Did You Know?

The Bible, especially the Hebrew Bible, uses the Hebrew root *qin'ah*, which is normally translated "jealous" or "zealous," to describe God. The word's root meaning conveys a deep passion and commitment for something or someone that leads to the desire to defend and protect. So when the Bible says that God is jealous, it is not in the sense of petty envy that we often associate with jealousy. When the Bible describes God as jealous, it means that he has a deep love for and commitment to his holiness and honor and an equally deep passion for his people.

---

1. Read 1 Kings 18:15–29. What do you notice about Elijah's boldness in speaking to King Ahab, the people of Israel, and the prophets of Baal?

   What level of commitment would be necessary to do and say these things? In other words, what motivated Elijah?

2. Read 1 Kings 18:30–40. How much physical effort did it take for Elijah to prepare the bull, build the altar, dig the trench? What does this tell you about his zeal for the Lord?

As you read Elijah's prayer, what do you see as the consuming passion of his heart? How much effort do you think it took to capture and execute the false prophets of Baal?

3. Read 1 Kings 18:41–46. Where did Elijah go after the false prophets were killed?

What did he do when it started raining? What does this tell you about the intensity of his passion and commitment to honor God?

Profile of a Zealous Servant

We do not know exactly where on Mount Carmel the events between Elijah and the prophets of Baal occurred, but we do know the Kishon River at its closest point is at least two miles and more than a thousand feet below the top of Mount Carmel. Elijah climbed Mount Carmel, built the stone altar, butchered a bull, descended to the Kishon River and supervised the execution of the prophets of Baal, climbed Mount Carmel again, descended the mountain, and ran ahead of King Ahab's chariot all the way to Jezreel more than eighteen miles away! That is one zealous servant of God! Even then, Elijah wasn't done. He went into the wilderness and for forty days and forty nights journeyed nearly two hundred miles across some of the most forbidding, mountainous desert in the world to reach Mount Horeb, the mountain of God (traditionally assumed to be Mount Sinai).

4. What does James 5:17–18 reveal about Elijah and our need to be passionately committed to God?

Is it possible for us to have the same passion as Elijah? Do you think God expects us to have that same zeal? Why or why not?

5. What surprises you about the disciples using metaphors of the Olympic games to describe an appropriate degree of passion for walking as Jesus walked? How well do you think it communicated the idea of the passion of Elijah to people in Roman colonies who had no idea who Elijah was?

6. Which metaphors do you think could communicate the passion of Elijah to people in our culture? How would you use those metaphors in describing your walk with Jesus?

ꜰaith Lesson (5 minutes)

First Kings 17 reveals an essential aspect of Elijah's zeal for God that we may tend to overlook if we focus exclusively on the powerful action and drama of 1 Kings 18. Read 1 Kings 17, taking special note of verses 1–5, 7–10, 13–14, and 17–24.

1. What kind of a relationship did Elijah have with God, and how did God's words—what God said to do—influence the prophet's words and actions?

2. What impact did Elijah's zeal and all-consuming passion to obey God in everything have on the widow of Zarephath (vv. 22–24)?

   In what ways is this similar to the impact Jesus and his disciples had on the people of their world?

3. Elijah was a man of God's Word. He knew it, honored it, quoted it, taught it, lived it, and challenged others to do the same. No wonder the first century Jews compared John the Baptist and Jesus to Elijah. They also knew God's Word and shared a common passion for it. How might people who know you describe your passion for the words of God?

4. How greatly do you desire to be zealous for God—to have the fire of Elijah in your heart? What kind of effort on your part is necessary to know and obey Gods words and become a passionate disciple of Jesus?

Worth Observing ...

Elijah is a remarkable example of a man who was zealously devoted to God, but he is just one of many faithful servants of God we can learn from in the Scriptures. Moses is another servant who served God zealously, and it is interesting to note the similarities between his life and Elijah's.

Moses	Elijah	Similar Life Experiences
Exodus 2:15	1 Kings 17:3	Fled a king and went east
Exodus 2:15–22	1 Kings 17:7–19	Stayed with a family
Exodus 16:8, 12	1 Kings 17:6	Was fed by God
Numbers 11:11–12	1 Kings 17:19–21	Complained about God's treatment
Exodus 3:1, 4, 10	1 Kings 18:1	Heard God's command to return to the land of the king
Exodus 7–12	1 Kings 18:20–39	Returned to confront a king and awaken faith in God's people
Exodus 24:4	1 Kings 18:30–31	Built/rebuilt an altar
Exodus 32:11–14	1 Kings 18:36–37	Prayed for God's people invoking Abraham, Isaac, and Israel
Exodus 32:25–29	1 Kings 18:37, 39–40	Sought confession, commitment, and the destruction of sin among the people

| Exodus 19–20 | 1 Kings 19 | Went to Mount Sinai (Horeb) and experienced God's appearance |
| Deuteronomy 1:37–38 | 1 Kings 19:16–21 | Appointed a successor whose name means "God [*Yahweh*] saves" (Joshua: "*Yahweh* saves"; Elisha: "God saves") |

closing (1 minute)

Read the following Scripture passage aloud, then pray, asking God to nurture the passion of Elijah in your hearts so that others will know that he is God.

Memorize

Therefore, since we are surrounded by such a great cloud of witnesses, let us throw off everything that hinders and the sin that so easily entangles, and let us run with perseverance the race marked out for us. Let us fix our eyes on Jesus, the author and perfecter of our faith, who for the joy set before him endured the cross, scorning its shame, and sat down at the right hand of the throne of God.

Hebrews 12:1–2

walk as jesus walked

In-Depth Personal Study Sessions

Day one/jesus and His Disciples: Displaying the zeal of Elijah

The Very Words of God

> *When Jesus came to the region of Caesarea Philippi, he asked his disciples, "Who do people say the Son of Man is?" They replied, "Some say John the Baptist; others say Elijah; and still others, Jeremiah or one of the prophets."*
>
> Matthew 16:13–14

Bible Discovery

Called to be Zealous for the Lord

The Jewish rabbis and their disciples (*talmidim*) sought to have the same fire, zeal, and passion for the Lord and his Word that Elijah modeled. As you will discover in the Scripture passages that follow, Jesus and his disciples did likewise. Not only that, the Lord expects no less from those who desire to be his disciples today. A disciple of Jesus must possess a fire for God, a passion for his Word, and the zeal to be an obedient follower who walks as Jesus walked.

1. As Jesus became better known and his reputation grew, who did people think he was? Why do you think they thought this, and what does it reveal about the kind of man Jesus was? (See Matthew 16:13–14; Mark 6:14–15.)

2. When he was in the temple before Passover, Jesus demonstrated his zeal for the Lord in a dramatic way. What did he do? Why? What impact did his words and actions have on people around him? (See John 2:13–22; also Psalm 69:9.)

Think About It

People who are passionate in their devotion to Jesus and seek to obey God in everything are often labeled as religious fanatics. Why? What is the difference between fanaticism and zeal? Is zeal for the Lord respected by the Christian community today?

---

3. The following Scripture passages highlight the kind of zeal for God that Jesus wants his disciples to have.

   a. Read Mark 8:34–38. What personal sacrifice must a person be willing to make to be a disciple of Jesus? Does this sacrifice require zeal for the Lord? Why or why not?

   b. Read Luke 9:57–62. Why do you think Jesus said what he did to these followers? What do you think Jesus was looking for in their response to him?

c. Read Mark 3:13–17. What indicates that at least some of Jesus' disciples were very zealous?

d. Read Luke 9:51–56. What evidence of zeal do we see in James and his brother, John? (Remember, fire from heaven is lightning in the Jewish understanding.) Who do you think they modeled themselves after? Where did they learn such zeal? (See 2 Kings 1:9–15.)

4. What evidence do the following passages provide that the early believers also were zealous for the Lord?

Scripture Passage	Zeal for the Lord Displayed
Acts 18:24–28	
Acts 21:10–15	
2 Cor. 8:16–22	
2 Cor. 9:1–2	
Col. 4:12–13	

Reflection

What, according to Romans 12:11, is expected of God's people? What do you think this means in your own daily walk with Jesus?

How do you think people who know you would describe your zeal for the Lord?

How do you think Jesus' disciples or the apostle Paul would describe your zeal in your walk with Jesus?

What do you do to maintain your spiritual fervor   the commitment to and enthusiasm for Jesus that his disciples had?

In what ways would you like to deepen your zeal for Jesus?

Paul gave the early believers practical instruction in how to be zealous for the Lord. Read carefully Galatians 4:18; Colossians 3:23–24; and Titus 2:11–14, then write down practical ways in which you can follow Paul's instructions in your daily life.

Memorize

Never be lacking in zeal, but keep your spiritual fervor, serving the Lord.

Romans 12:11

Day Two/Zealous to Obey and Honor God

The Very Words of God

In those days John the Baptist came, preaching in the Desert of Judea and saying, "Repent, for the kingdom of heaven is near." ... People went out to him from Jerusalem and all Judea and the whole region of the Jordan. Confessing their sins, they were baptized by him in the Jordan River.

Matthew 3:1–2, 5–6

Bible Discovery

Zealous to Fulfill the Word of God

The ministry of John the Baptist focused on preparing people for the coming of Messiah and God's great acts of redemption. John was widely recognized as having the same passion for God that Elijah had, and he was deeply committed to the Hebrew Scriptures as the basis for his teaching and actions. So take a closer look at John's zeal for God and see how God greatly used him to warn people of God's judgment and bring them to repentance in preparation for the coming of Messiah.

Did You Know?

John must have known he was the fulfillment of the Malachi 4 prophecy—the Elijah to come. From his knowledge of the Hebrew text, John knew where key events in Elijah's life occurred, and he often chose "Elijah places" in which to baptize people:

- The vicinity of the Judean wilderness, near Jericho, probably near the fords of the Jordan (2 Kings 2:3–14; Matthew 3:1–6).
- At Aenon, in the vicinity of Beth Shean, near where Elijah called Elisha (Meholah) (1 Kings 19:15–18; John 3:23).
- At Bethany beyond the Jordan, near the Yarmuk River, believed to be the brook Kerith where Elijah hid from Ahab* (1 Kings 17:1–5; John 1:19–28).

The area of ministry of John the Baptist

*Bargil Pixner, *The Fifth Gospel: With Jesus Through Galilee*. Rosh Pina, Israel. Corazin Publishing, 1992, 19–21; Rami Arav, *Bethsaida*. Kirksville, Mo.: Truman State University Press, 1999, vol. 2, 388–390.

1. According to Malachi's prophecies (3:1; 4:1–6), who would pre-
    cede the Messiah's coming—known by the Jews as the "day of
    the Lord"—and what would his task be?

2. What message did the angel of God give to Zechariah as he was
    burning incense in the temple? What did the angel say about
    John's zeal for God? (See Luke 1:8–17.)

3. How do we know that Jesus considered John to be the Elijah
    who would come as promised by the prophet Malachi? How
    did Jesus view John and his ministry? (See Matthew 3:13–15;
    11:7–14; 17:10–13.)

4. Who did the religious leaders think John might be? What was
    their response to him? (See John 1:19–28.)

5. What do each of the following passages reveal about the zeal of
    John the Baptist? How far was he willing to go, and how much
    was he willing to sacrifice, to be who God had called him to be?
    How zealous was he to proclaim the message of God?

    a.   Matthew 3:1–4 (see also 2 Kings 1:8)

    b.   Matthew 3:5–12

    c.   Mark 1:1–4

    d.   Mark 6:17–20

The desolate Wilderness of Judah where John the Baptist ministered

Phinehas: Zealous for God's Honor

Numbers 25:1–13 records the shocking story of Israel's seduction by Moab and its shameless digression into sexual immorality and worship of Baal. Moses told the people of Israel that the Lord commanded them to kill everyone who had participated in these activities. Yet, in direct disobedience to God, an Israelite man took a Moabite woman into his tent and presumably had sexual relations with her. This happened right in front of Moses, right in front of the tabernacle where God's presence lived!

This was too much for Phinehas, grandson of Aaron, the priest. Displaying passionate zeal for God's honor, Phinehas went into the tent and drove a spear through both the Israelite and the Moabite woman. God commended Phinehas for zealously upholding his honor and rewarded him with a covenant of a lasting priesthood.

Phinehas and his zeal for the Lord is still remembered today. His zeal for God was immortalized in Psalm 106:28–31, and the Zealots considered him a hero and a model. The zeal Phinehas showed in preserving God's honor in the face of idolatry is quite similar to that of Elijah, so it is no wonder that rabbinic literature often discusses Phinehas and Elijah together.

Reflection

Those who are zealous for God make an impact on people not only during their lifetime, but often for generations—even millennia—to come. Just think of how many people today know of Moses and Elijah, of Peter and Paul, and to a lesser extent Phinehas and John the Baptist. Read Acts 19:1–9, which records an encounter the apostle Paul had with some of John's disciples in Ephesus—nearly seven hundred miles from Israel—and consider the following questions.

What does the presence of these disciples in Ephesus indicate about the impact John's zeal for God had on others? How zealous do you think these disciples were, and who were they trying to imitate when Paul met them?

Whose disciples did John's disciples become after Paul told them about Jesus? What does this tell you about their knowledge of Scripture and their zeal for obeying it?

How much does the Christian community today desire the zeal of Elijah? How much do we seek to be filled with passionate devotion and obedience to Christ and the Scriptures? How much of an impact do we have on the world around us?

How important is it to you to be zealous for God? For how long do you want the world to remember your zeal for God?

DAY THREE/sharing the passion of Elijah

The Very Words of God

Always be zealous for the fear of the LORD.

Proverbs 23:17

Bible Discovery

Teaching Elijah's Passion to People Who Never Knew Him

To zealously love God is to love him with one's whole being, and godly people of every era and culture have a consuming passion to do his will and maintain his honor in everything they do and say. The Jews of Jesus' day had been taught of Elijah's passion from their earliest days, so they readily understood what it meant to zealously walk with God. But what about the people of Asia Minor who were immersed in the pagan, Hellenistic culture of the Roman Empire? They had no knowledge of Elijah. They aspired to pleasure and self-preservation. How would Jesus' disciples teach them to walk as Jesus walked?

In the arena of athletics and the Olympic games, Jesus' disciples and biblical writers found powerful metaphors of the zeal God desires. The games were widely known throughout the Roman world, and the biblical writers used the metaphors of athletic training and performance to communicate the gospel message. By capturing images of the intensity, passion, and focus required for athletic competition, they were able to explain true discipleship to people who were otherwise unfamiliar with God and his Word.

1. Even before God called him to preach the news of Christ to the Gentiles, Paul was extremely zealous for God. What things does he reveal about himself that show he took this calling seriously? Which metaphor did he use to describe his walk with Jesus? What were his concerns regarding his performance? (See Galatians 1:13–2:2, especially 2:2.)

2. Read 2 Timothy 2:1–5. Which two metaphors that would have been very familiar to people of the Roman Empire did Paul use to

encourage Timothy in his walk with Jesus? How intense a focus and commitment does this tell us Paul expected of Timothy?

3. In Galatians 5:7–8, Paul told the Galatians that they had been "running a good race." What apparently happened to them and how did Paul "coach" them regarding the importance of their effort?

4. What did Paul hope for his disciples, and what would it mean to him? In what way does this illustrate that he was walking as Jesus walked? (See Philippians 2:14–16.)

5. Which images did Paul use to picture his life of faith? What does this tell us about the way he approached his "walk" as a disciple of Jesus? Do you think he was running a sprint or a marathon? (See 2 Timothy 4:6–8.)

Did You Know?

During the first century, the winners of athletic games would each receive a wreath of olive branches or even gold, which imitated the wreath the gods were portrayed as wearing. The wreath was given in honor of the athletes' faithfulness and exceptional performance, much like an Olympic champion today would receive a gold medal.

In keeping with the athletic competition metaphor they often used to describe the Christian walk, the New Testament writers used the Greek word *stephanos* (crown) to describe the reward righteous people will receive for their faithfulness to God. This word typically refers to the winners' wreath presented during the games as opposed to the word *diadem* (also translated as crown) that is used only in reference to Jesus (Revelation 19:12) and the Devil (Revelation 12:3).

On our own, none of us deserves to receive a wreath of honor. But by God's grace, Scripture's guidance, the encouragement of the faith community, and the gift of the Holy Spirit, God forgives us for our failures. He enables us to be faithful and promises to reward our faithfulness. So we must *run*—not walk, not jog, but *run*—as we live for him!

6. What zeal and passion does Paul demonstrate as he coaches the Corinthians in how to live and train for obedience to God? In what ways did Paul demonstrate this dedication in his own life? (See 1 Corinthians 9:24–27.)

7. Which images of your world do you think communicate the zealous nature of being a disciple of Jesus in your culture?

Reflection

The idea of living zealously for God doesn't come solely from the New Testament writers, from Jesus' disciples, or even from the prophet Elijah or the patriarch Moses; it comes from God himself. Scripture frequently describes God as being zealous—intensely passionate—about everything he does, and he expects his people to respond to him by imitating his zeal and returning his love. Read Deuteronomy 29:14–29 and Isaiah 9:1–2, 6–7, which describe the nature, the fervor, and the intent of God's zeal.

Why does God desire us to be zealous for him and his Word?

In what ways does a greater understanding of God's zealous nature influence your walk with Jesus?

How zealously are you "running" your "race" for Jesus? Is your effort best described as a sprint or a marathon? How committed are you to "running to win"?

Memorize

Run in such a way as to get the prize.

1 Corinthians 9:24

Data File

Aphrodisias — A Culture Far Removed from God

Located in the Meander River Valley (150 miles from Ephesus and less than 50 miles from Laodicea and Colosse), Aphrodisias in the first century was a typical Greek/Roman city of about thirty thousand people. Founded by the Carians before Abraham's time (c. 1600 BC), the city was initially named Ninoe after the local fertility goddess who was also known as Ashera. The city came under Greek influence in about 1000 BC, and the Greek goddess Aphrodite replaced the ancient Ninoe. During the Greek period, the city became known as a cultural center and location for one of the ancient world's great schools of sculpture. Many of the magnificent statues and carvings found in archaeological digs around the Mediterranean world can be traced to the stone or sculptors of Aphrodisias.

The ceremonial gate, called the Tetrapylon, of what remains of the temple of Aphrodite in Aphrodisias. In the background, only fourteen of the original forty columns of the temple remain standing. The gate in the foreground displays some of the fine, detailed sculpture for which the city was known.

From a religious standpoint, Aphrodite (the goddess of love, beauty, seduction, and sexual pleasure) was the dominant deity in Aphrodisias. Also called "the Queen of Heaven," she represented frivolity, promiscuity, and sexual pleasure without commitment. Worship of Aphrodite celebrated her unfaithfulness to her "ordinary" husband, Hephaestus, and her promise of fertility, love, and sexual fulfillment made her very popular.

Aphrodisias came under the Roman Empire in 20 BC during the reign of Caesar Augustus. The temple to Augustus, the Sebasteion built as a center for worship of the Roman emperors, the Portico of Tiberius in the agora (city marketplace), and the bath complex built by Hadrian indicate the wealth, influence, and power of the city during the Roman period. In addition to these structures, the city had a forum, theater, and arena.

Although Paul traveled through the Meander River Valley and John wrote Revelation, in part, to the church at nearby Laodicea, Aphrodisias is not mentioned in the Bible. However, we do know that the city had a Jewish community and a very early Christian community. Imagine the zeal the Christians in this city must have had in order to walk as Jesus walked!

Day four/acclaiming the greatness of god!

The Very Words of God

Do you not know that in a race all the runners run, but only one gets the prize? . . . Therefore I do not run like a man running aimlessly; I do not fight like a man beating the air. No, I beat my body and make it my slave so that after I have preached to others, I myself will not be disqualified for the prize.

1 Corinthians 9:24, 26–27

Bible Discovery

The Sacrifice of Passionate Devotion to God

The athletic competition and games metaphors used by the early Christian disciples were more than just a meaningful way to communicate the passion of Elijah to people who had never heard of him. In the Roman Empire, running the race of faith was also an acclamation of loyalty that would become a matter of life and death for the early believers. This is because the Roman emperors considered themselves to be divine and became increasingly insistent that their subjects acclaim and honor their deity. The Scripture study beginning on page 40 explores the passion of the early believers in the face of emperor worship.

Fact File
Games of Life and Death

Emperor worship was increasingly a fact of life in the Roman Empire from the reign of Caesar Augustus onward. As the empire became more and more diverse with multitudes of gods and religions, worship of the emperor as god became a vital form of unification. The people could worship their respective gods freely as long as they would also publicly declare that "Caesar is Lord."

Any civic celebration in the Roman world was, in fact, a religious activity. The theater, city council, gladiatorial combat, and oratorical or artistic competitions were all religious events. Festivities began with animal offerings, incense, and dedications to the gods of the event. Choirs sang praises to the deities of the community and to the empire. Each event was a form of worship performed as an offering to honor the gods.

Competition in the Olympic games, which had largely become the Imperial games, was also considered an offering to the gods, a testimony to the greatness of the deity in whose name the athletes performed. Over time, the games became the stage from which spectators and participants alike could acclaim the emperor's deity and affirm their loyalty to him. Spectators by the

---

thousands (the stadium in Aphrodisias seated 30,000–35,000) would cheer as the emperor and his officials entered the stadium and took their places in the royal box. The athletes then dedicated their performance to their gods and competed to honor the emperor's lordship and to acclaim his deity.

The stadium of Aphrodisias, site of the Imperial games

This created a dilemma for Jews and Christians alike who would not worship any other gods. Knowing that the Jews would never acclaim the deity of the Roman emperor, Herod had persuaded Caesar Augustus to grant the Jews an exemption from the emperor worship requirement. The community of Jesus did not have such an exemption, however, and the early Christians experienced great pressure to participate in processions, festivals, and games to acclaim the emperor as god and to affirm their loyalty to him. Many of them, including nearly all of Jesus' disciples, had to make the ultimate choice—to sacrifice their lives, or to deny Jesus as their Lord and King and live.

1. What did Paul write to Timothy as the pressure of emperor worship intensified? What evidence of the passion of Elijah do you see in his words? How do you think Timothy and the people he pastored in Ephesus responded? (See 1 Timothy 6:11–16.)

2. What did believers who faced the harsh reality of emperor worship — the possibility they could be put to death for acclaiming Jesus alone — learn about the hope of their commitment to the lordship of Jesus Christ from Romans 10:9–11; Philippians 2:5–11; and 1 Peter 3:13–18, 22? How would these words have fueled their passion?

**The Sebasteion of Aphrodisias,
where the emperors of Rome were worshiped**

3. The emperor's authority as ruler and the reality of emperor worship in the Roman Empire during the time of Jesus sheds an interesting light on the interaction between Jesus and Pilate prior to Jesus' crucifixion. Read John 18:28–37; 19:7–16 and consider what lines were being drawn, what loyalties were being affirmed, and what the future implications would be.

a. Who sentenced Jesus to death, and what authority did he represent?

b. Why do you think Jesus submitted himself to the authority of a Roman emperor who claimed to be god? How do you think the early Christians who faced death because of their obedience to God viewed what Jesus did?

c. What were the implications of Pilate's actions (as the emperor's representative) for the early believers as they faced the pressure to acknowledge the emperor as Lord?

d. What were the implications of Jesus' claim to be the Son of God that so greatly offended the Jews? What do you think were the implications of the chief priests' statement to Pilate that they had no king but Caesar?

4. After his resurrection, Jesus spent forty days with his disciples
    proving that he was alive, teaching them about the kingdom of
    God, and instructing them in what they were to do. Read Acts
    1:3–11 and answer the following questions.

    a. What "mission" did Jesus give his disciples? Of what were
        they witnesses?

    b. In light of the growing emphasis on emperor worship, why
        do you think it was important that Jesus' disciples saw him
        ascend into heaven?

    c. What connection would the disciples have made between
        Daniel 7:13–14, 27 and what they had seen? How do you think
        it would have affected their zeal for being Jesus' witnesses?

The Truth of the Matter
Who Is Lord?

A Roman emperor was declared divine when witnesses
claimed to have seen the emperor's father ascend to heaven, thus
making the emperor the "Son of God." This process was called
apotheosis. The emperor's deity stood on the validity of these witnesses. Augustus, for example declared his father, Julius, divine
in 29 BC and a statue of Julius was placed in the Prytaneion in
Ephesus. Augustus then declared himself "Son of God," and the
Senate affirmed the declaration.

> In contrast, consider who witnessed Jesus' ascension, who the disciples told about his ascension, and/or how people responded to the news. See Acts 1:1–9; 2:14, 32–36, 41; 7:55–58; and Hebrews 1:1–12; 8:1; 12:2.

Reflection

Jesus' first disciples did not know that most of them eventually would give their lives to be witnesses of his lordship, but when the time came, they did. If you are going to be his witness, you do not know what the future holds either.

> To what extent are you committed to "run the race" to honor him? How far are you willing to go to be the kind of witness Jesus' disciples were? Would you give your life?

> What do you think gave the early followers of Jesus the courage to stand up for him rather than worship the emperor? What gives you that courage, particularly in the face of opposition?

> A significant part of the believer's task is to declare the lordship of Jesus in everyday life. How do you do this? What more is required of you to do it with the commitment and intensity of an athlete who is competing to win the prize?

When Your Life Is on the Line

Walking as Jesus walked in cities of the Roman Empire such as Aphrodisias required intense dedication and unwavering passion to obey God in everything. What fueled the passion of the early disciples to give everything they had—even life itself—to honor and acclaim Jesus as their Savior and Son of God?

The Demands of Emperor Worship	What Fueled the Disciples' Passion
The emperor claimed to be divine.	1 Timothy 6:12–16; 1 Corinthians 8:5–6
You are asked to sprinkle incense during a festival to acknowledge the emperor's deity and authority.	Romans 10:9; Philippians 2:5–11
No one believes that Jesus is Lord and the Son of God.	1 John 4:2–3
You fear the severe penalty for not acknowledging the emperor's deity.	1 John 4:4; 1 Peter 5:10–11; Revelation 13:10
You are tempted to remain silent about your belief in Jesus.	1 Peter 3:13–17
You are not allowed to conduct business, get water from public fountains, or participate in city life.	Revelation 13:1, 4–8, 11–17

Day five/A personal challenge

The Very Words of God

Therefore, since we are surrounded by such a great cloud of witnesses, let us throw off everything that hinders and the sin that so easily entangles, and let us run with perseverance the race marked out for us.

Hebrews 12:1

Bible Discovery

The Great Cloud of Witnesses

The stadium in Aphrodisias is a dramatic reminder of the passion with which we are to train, compete, and fight to "run" our walk of discipleship with Jesus with all of our heart, soul, and strength. But that is not all. As Ray Vander Laan pointed out, the stadium is also a reminder of the crowds of faithful followers of God who have gone before us. They already have fought the good fight, acclaimed their Lord and King, and won the prize of his everlasting honor. We can think of them as the witnesses of our walk, our faith, our "race." They are, in a sense, our "fans" who cheer us on as we remember their faithfulness to our Lord.

1. Read Hebrews 11:1 – 12:1. Read it more than once so that you take in more of its meaning and significance.

   a. Which great men and/or women of faith mentioned in Hebrews 11:1 – 31 stood out to you? Why?

   b. Who comprises the "great cloud of witnesses" who have run the race before us?

c. Faith for these witnesses involved far more than verbal assent or even rational belief in God and his Word. What was it that made their faith commendable?

d. How much effort, passion, and zeal for God did these witnesses demonstrate?

e. What can we learn from them about what it means to "run" the race for Jesus? And why must we do this?

Think About It

We must view faith in God as a race. It is more than intellectual assent. It is *belief* that we put into action during a marathon-like race to grow more like Jesus, one we can picture being run in front of previous runners of God's race of faith who have finished their earthly races.

2. According to Hebrews 12:2–3, what motivated Jesus, and what did he do? What effect should his example have on us?

3. If we have a mental picture of life being like a marathon that we are running in front of great runners of God's race of faith who have gone before us, how might that change how we live—and the effort we expend running our "race"?

Did You Know?

One of the most significant finds in the ruins of Aphrodisias is a simple marble pillar, called a stele, that has legible inscriptions (in Greek) on two of its four faces. It is believed the pillar dates from the time period during which the early church was growing in Aphrodisias. Scholars also are quite certain that the pillar is associated with a synagogue or a charitable undertaking, most likely a soup kitchen or food pantry, of the synagogue community.

 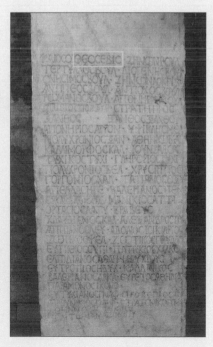

The lists on the pillar are intriguing. One face lists individuals who have contributed to the construction of a new building. The other face (the main one) lists people associated with the project. The first group of fifty-five names are under the heading "Jews," and the list designates three proselytes or converts, meaning three Gentiles who had fully converted to Judaism (including circumcision). The second portion of the list is under the heading "*theosebes*," which means God-fearers (the word is highlighted in the photo on page 47). These apparently were Gentiles who had been attracted to God by the faithful living of the Jewish community and, although they had not completely converted to Judaism, had abandoned their pagan gods and practices in order to obey and honor the God of the Bible and associate with the Jewish community.

Even before the Christian message came to the Roman world, God had been drawing pagan Gentiles to himself! To see the pillar at Aphrodisias with its list of fifty-five God-fearers is to see passionate devotion to God in action. How could any of these witnesses have imagined that their faith in God would speak to their world and still speak so powerfully today? We can find great encouragement in the fact that if we live faithfully and speak clearly of our love for Jesus, God has and is always preparing an audience that is eager to hear the good news.

Reflection

Which "witness" or hero of the faith mentioned in Hebrews 11 (or a spouse, parent, brother, sister, child, or friend who has impacted your life) cheers you on as you remember how faithfully he or she ran the race God had set out?

What about that person's faith challenges or encourages you? Write down what that person's example teaches you and what you want to emulate in your walk with Jesus.

In what ways does remembering the life and example of this person help you to run more faithfully?

What kind of a "witness" are you to other believers? What is it about the way you run your race that can help them run their best races for Jesus?

Which things "hinder" and "entangle" you as you seek to "run" more faithfully for Jesus? What must you do to eliminate them from your life?

Speak to God about your admiration for faithful believers around the world who put their lives on the line because they believe in Jesus. Ask him to give you an unquenchable desire to demonstrate your commitment to the lordship of Jesus.

Memorize

Let us fix our eyes on Jesus, the author and perfecter of our faith, who for the joy set before him endured the cross, scorning its shame, and sat down at the right hand of the throne of God. Consider him who endured such opposition from sinful men, so that you will not grow weary and lose heart.

Hebrews 12:2–3

Declare God's Lordship Over Your Life!

- Jesus is Lord and God, not anyone else.
- God has declared that he alone is Lord and in control.
- All Christians—and saints who lived zealously for God—are God's Olympians.
- Your walk with and for God as his disciple is a declaration of God's lordship in your everyday world.
- You are called to live for God, not yourself.

Learning to walk like Jesus: paul's journey to rome

There is probably no greater hero of the Christian faith than the apostle Paul. He was a passionate disciple of Jesus the Messiah and the most successful early messenger to take the good news about Jesus beyond the land of Israel. He was an exceptional Hebrew Bible scholar and an articulate speaker and writer. He traveled relentlessly and courageously shared his faith in Jesus wherever he went, always praising the God he worshiped.

Just as Moses and Elijah were great prophets of God in the Jewish community of the Old Testament, Paul was a great prophet of Jesus in Christian communities of the Roman world. Much of the New Testament was either written about him (Acts) or came from his Spirit-inspired writing. Paul effectively carried God's message to the Roman world, and he remains an excellent role model for all of Jesus' followers today.

Like each of us, Paul had to learn to become like Jesus, his Rabbi. In one sense, Paul had a tremendous head start on us. He had memorized much, if not all, of the Hebrew Bible and had been educated as a disciple of Gamaliel — the greatest Jewish scholar of the day. So before he even met Jesus, Paul knew what it meant to be a disciple, to become a rabbi, and to make disciples.

After Jesus encountered Paul on the road to Damascus, Paul became utterly convinced that Jesus was God's Messiah. He immediately began preaching the message of Jesus in the synagogues of Damascus. He longed to take the gospel message to the heart of the Roman Empire. But before God allowed him to go to Rome, Paul needed to learn to walk as Jesus walked. He needed to learn how to take on the yoke of the Torah—to learn to reinterpret his vast understanding of the Hebrew Bible in light of Jesus—and to make disciples in the way Jesus made disciples.

This session focuses on Paul's early teaching ministry. We will discover his passion to share his faith with everyone—Jews and Gentiles. We will see his intense devotion to God as he slowly discovers God's will for his life and work. We will learn from his Jewish way of sharing the message of Jesus that, through God's blessing, would change the world. And we will be challenged to imitate Paul's willingness to place God's plans and desires ahead of his own even though he wanted with all his heart to take the message of Jesus to Rome.

So let's begin. Let's learn to walk as Jesus walked by allowing Paul to be our teacher and rabbi, just as he became teacher and rabbi for believers in the ancient city of Antioch of Pisidia and other locations in the remote Roman province of Galatia.

opening Thoughts (4 minutes)

The Very Words of God

God, who set me apart from birth and called me by his grace, was pleased to reveal his Son in me so that I might preach him among the Gentiles.

Galatians 1:15–16

Think About It

When we truly believe that God wants us to do something and are committed to the calling, how do we tend to respond? How much effort are we willing to put into preparing for what God would have us do? How long are we willing to wait for God's timing?

DVD Notes (23 minutes)

Caesar's temple by the Damascus road

Paul meets Jesus

Antioch of Pisidia — a miniature Rome

Paul goes out to teach the kingdom of God

DVD Highlights (4 minutes)

1. What were your impressions of Antioch of Pisidia — a miniature
   Rome in the mountains of rural, wild Galatia?

What do you think it would have been like to live in that beautiful, cultured city that was so far removed and also so closely aligned with the power center of the Roman Empire?

2. What do you think Paul thought when he arrived in Antioch and saw the tetrastyle temple of Caesar Augustus — nearly identical to the temple of Caesar Augustus in Omrit that stood near the Damascus Road where Paul met Jesus?

In what ways might the dominant presence of Caesar's temple in Antioch have influenced Paul as he ministered there?

3. The Jewish community and synagogue played a significant role in Paul's teaching in Antioch. What impact — positive as well as negative — did the Jewish community have on his ministry?

What does this tell you about the nature of the Jewish community in Antioch?

small group bible discovery and discussion (18 minutes)

Paul's Message, Paul's Mission

Paul, a zealously devout Jew, knew without a doubt that he had been called by God "who set me apart from birth and called me by his grace" to preach the gospel of Jesus to the Gentiles (see Galatians 1:11–16, particularly verse 15). He considered his call to be similar to that of such Hebrew prophets as Isaiah, Jeremiah, and Ezekiel. After all, Jesus himself had revealed Paul's message and mission to him. So let's follow Paul (or Saul, as he was still known at the time) as he begins his first ministry tour. He and his companions began teaching in the synagogues of Cyprus, then moved on to the province of Galatia in Asia Minor.

Data File
Paul's First Teaching Tour

Paul and Barnabas took their first teaching tour through the region of Galatia in about AD 46–48. Highlights of their journey, recorded in Acts 13–14, include:

- A stop on the island of Cyprus, where Paul met Sergius Paulus, who became his first convert.
- Sailing from Cyprus to Perga, then walking more than a hundred miles through difficult terrain to Antioch of Pisidia.
- Teaching in the synagogue in Antioch where many people gladly received the message of the kingdom of God.
- Walking seventy-five miles to Iconium after those who opposed their message in Antioch influenced the leaders to have Paul and Barnabas expelled from the city.
- Teaching in Iconium for some time until they learned of a plot to kill them.

- Leaving Iconium and walking across about fifty miles of rugged terrain to Lystra, where they continued to preach the good news.
- Walking another one hundred miles to Derbe after those who had opposed them in Antioch and Iconium incited the crowd in Lystra to stone Paul.
- Preaching the good news and winning many more disciples in Derbe.
- Retracing their route through Lystra, Iconium, Antioch, and Perga (more than 325 miles!), in order to encourage disciples along the way.
- Sailing back to their starting point, Antioch in Syria, then walking to Jerusalem.

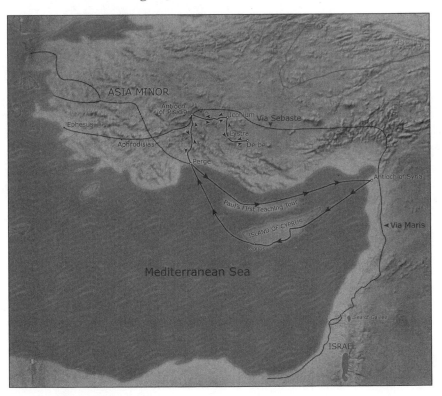

1. How did Paul, Barnabas, and the early community of believers know that God had chosen these two men to be his messengers? What were they to do? (See Acts 9:15–22; 13:1–4.)

2. After teaching on the island of Cyprus, Paul and Barnabas met Sergius Paulus, a powerful and influential Roman official who became a believer. (It is at this time Saul took the name Paul.) Then the two headed straight for Antioch of Pisidia, a miniature Rome tucked away in rural Galatia. They entered the synagogue, where the leaders asked Paul to speak to the worshipers. His message is recorded in Acts 13:16–41. Read the verses and discuss the following questions.

    a. What was the essence of Paul's message? Of what and whom did Paul testify? (Hint: who is doing the action in this passage?)

    b. To whom did Paul address this message? (See verses 16, 26.) Why is this significant? What is Paul saying about God's message of salvation?

    c. Discuss which aspects of Paul's message would have been especially meaningful to his Jewish listeners. Which aspects of the message would have been especially meaningful to the God-fearing Gentiles who worshiped with the Jews?

3. Paul's message so impressed the synagogue congregation that
    nearly the whole city showed up on the next Sabbath to hear
    him speak, leading some Jews to speak against Paul. Read how
    Paul and Barnabas responded in Acts 13:46–49.

    a. What major shift was taking place in the mission of pro-
        claiming God's message of salvation? Do you think Paul and
        Barnabas anticipated this? Explain your answer.

    b. How do you think these events, particularly the Gentiles'
        response, influenced Paul's passion to press on with the mis-
        sion God had given to him?

    c. As Paul and Barnabas left Antioch of Pisidia and headed
        toward Iconium, what might they have discussed regarding
        the message and mission God had given to them in rela-
        tionship to their experiences on the island of Cyprus and
        in Antioch? What may have amazed them? Thrilled them?
        Grieved them?

faith Lesson: (5 minutes)

Jesus gave Paul a specific message and a mission to fulfill. Before
ascending to heaven, Jesus gave each of his disciples a message and

mission as well. It is recorded in Matthew 28:18–20. Read this passage and consider how you are carrying out that calling.

1. How well would you be able to give a message such as Paul's sermon recorded in Acts 13, using no notes or Scripture in hand, that would be filled with Bible stories, allusions, and quotations? What made Paul's teaching so powerful and effective?

2. What makes God's message powerful and effective today? What must you do to become more like Jesus in your ability to fill your speech and the witness of your daily life with the message and Word of God?

3. What excites you about the opportunities God is giving you to be his witness—at home, in your neighborhood and workplace, and so on? What is holding you back from speaking boldly for Jesus and walking as he walked?

closing (1 minute)

Read aloud the verses on page 60. Then pray, asking God to give you a deep commitment to prepare yourself (no matter what your age) for the ministry that lies ahead of you. Pray that you will be as ready and eager to take up God's calling—whatever it is—as Paul was.

Memorize

While they were worshiping the Lord and fasting, the Holy Spirit said, "Set apart for me Barnabas and Saul for the work to which I have called them." So after they had fasted and prayed, they placed their hands on them and sent them off.

Acts 13:2–3

walk as jesus walked

In-Depth Personal Study Sessions

Day one/why Antioch of pisidia?

The Very Words of God

I planned many times to come to you (but have been prevented from doing so until now) in order that I might have a harvest among you, just as I have had among the other Gentiles. I am obligated both to Greeks and non-Greeks, both to the wise and the foolish. That is why I am so eager to preach the gospel also to you who are at Rome.

Romans 1:13–15

Bible Discovery

Paul's Pursuit of Rome

We know that Paul had a deep desire to go to Rome and that for many years God prevented him from doing so. Yet Rome was never far from Paul's thoughts. Although we don't know for sure, Paul's desire to take God's message to Rome may be part of the reason he visited the remote city of Antioch of Pisidia during his first teaching journey.

The city of Antioch of Pisidia was designed like a miniature Rome. It was home to a number of powerful and influential families in the Roman Empire, including the family of Sergius Paulus, Paul's first known convert. Why did Paul go there? Perhaps Sergius Paulus helped him contact influential Romans who lived there. Or, like many new believers who are anxious for their loved ones to hear the message of Jesus, Sergius Paulus may have asked Paul to go to Antioch to share the message with his family. Or, Paul may have thought that by speaking to Romans in Antioch he would be influencing Rome as well. In any case, take a closer look at Paul's desire to preach the message of Jesus in Rome and the link to Antioch of Pisidia.

1. Paul wrote about his desire to go to Rome in Romans 1:8–15. How badly did he want to go there and why?

2. As Barnabas and Paul taught on the island of Cyprus, who became a believer? What impact did this man's conversion seem to have on Paul? (See Acts 13:4–12.)

Profile of Sergius Paulus

Sergius Paulus, Paul's first known convert, was one of the highest-ranking officials of the entire Roman Empire! He is known from Roman history and archaeological research as a confidante of the Imperial Court in Rome. As proconsul (think in terms of a cabinet-level position today), he was just below Emperor Claudius in status. He came from Antioch of Pisidia, and his family had large land holdings and estates in the vicinity.

---

3. Paul knew that he was to take the gospel message to the Gentiles. (See Acts 9:15.) In what ways might the conversion of Sergius Paulus have influenced Paul's desire to bring God's message to the highest levels of the Roman Empire? To Antioch of Pisidia?

Did You Know?

Why did Saul become known as Paul? Many scholars believe that Saul took the last name of Sergius Paulus (in Greek, *Paul* is *Paulus*), an uncommon Roman family name, to gain contacts with Imperial Rome. His new name gave Paul a significant identity in the Roman world, but notice that God did not change his Jewish name.

---

4. Acts 13 records the visit of Paul and Barnabas to Antioch of Pisidia, a key center of Roman influence.

    a. When Paul spoke in Antioch, what kinds of people were in his audience and heard his message? (See Acts 13:16, 26, 43–44, 48.)

    b. When Paul and Barnabas spoke on the Sabbath for the second time, who showed up to hear them? What kind of excitement did their presence and message stir up? What kind of interest do you think these events may have generated in the upper levels of Roman society? (See Acts 13:44–50.)

5. For many years, God made it clear to Paul that he was not to go to Rome. When and how did Paul know that God would allow him to fulfill his life's desire to go to Rome and testify of God's message of salvation? (See Acts 23:11; Romans 15:18–24.)

Data File
Antioch of Pisidia

- Founded by Antiochus I, a Greek successor of Alexander the Great, during the third century BC.
- Reestablished in about 25 BC by Caesar Augustus as part of his attempt to Romanize the area. He made it a military colony of veteran Roman Legionnaires (Roman Marines).
- Was the largest city (estimated 10,000 – 12,000 people) in the remote Roman province of Galatia (now Turkey).
- Was home to many prominent Romans, including Nero's father.

Remains of the aqueduct that carried fresh water into Antioch of Pisidia

- Designed to be a smaller version of Rome itself, the city was divided into seven sections with the same names as the seven hills of Rome. It had many features commonly found in Roman cities including: a semicircular theater that seated 15,000 people and had space for an orchestra; a spring-fed reservoir and aqueduct system that provided fresh water from the mountains more than six miles away; and paved streets that were not the norm in remote Galatia. Its most outstanding feature, however, was a large temple dedicated to Caesar Augustus that was probably built by Tiberius.

The paved streets of Antioch of Pisidia, a luxury the Romans brought to the city, were a marked contrast to the unpaved streets usually found in the small villages of Galatia.

* Although the city was on the *Via Sebaste*, the main trade route between Persia and Rome, it remained fairly isolated due to its distance from other major cities — nearly 270 miles by road to Ephesus and 700 miles to Jerusalem.
* Had a significant Jewish community and synagogue, was a key location for Paul's ministry, and eventually became predominantly Christian.

Reflection

Read again Acts 13:46 – 51 and write down all the ways you see Paul saying and doing the kinds of things Jesus would say and do. To what extent was Paul walking as Jesus walked?

What impact did the message of the kingdom of God have on the people of Antioch of Pisidia?

What does Paul's decision to go to Rome only when God permits it say to you about his commitment to become like Jesus?

How willing are you to follow God's path and walk as Jesus walked even when you passionately desire to take another path?

Day Two/Challenging the Lordship of Caesar

The Very Words of God

Pray also for me, that whenever I open my mouth, words may be given me so that I will fearlessly make known the mystery of the gospel, for which I am an ambassador in chains. Pray that I may declare it fearlessly, as I should.

Ephesians 6:19 – 20

Bible Discovery

Paul Confronts Imperial Rome

Paul had great passion to declare and defend God's honor, and he wanted to share the message of Jesus with everyone — Jew and Gentile, small and great. He even wanted to take the message of Jesus to Rome, to the heart and power center of the Roman Empire. God had more for Paul to learn and other things for him to do before he made that one-way trip, however. So for years God prevented Paul from going to Rome.

But God placed no limits on how powerfully Paul undermined the deity of the Roman emperor by teaching about the salvation that Jesus the Son of God freely offers to everyone. So Paul faithfully proclaimed the lordship of Christ by his teaching and by the way he lived every day. With no fear of human authority or power, he taught the message of Jesus everywhere he went, even in places like Antioch of Pisidia, which was a center for emperor worship.

The remains of the temple of Caesar in Antioch and how it once looked (inset). Imagine what a stunning reflection of the emperor's power and glory it must have been in Paul's day.

1. When Paul taught in the synagogue in Antioch, he was probably within sight of Caesar's temple on the hill overlooking the city. Yet there is no indication that he "softened" his message to placate the Roman authorities.

    a. Which points in Paul's sermon would Rome have considered to be treasonous? (See Acts 13:23, 27, 30–34, 46–47.)

    b. What stinging words concerning Roman authority did Paul use? (Especially note verses 27–28 of the same passage.)

2. No matter where he went in the Roman Empire, Paul taught about the kingdom of God and boldly declared the lordship of Christ. Read each of the Scripture passages below and note how Paul denied the emperor's deity and lordship.

    a. Romans 1:1–4. Who did Paul say Jesus is? Who was Jesus to Paul?

    b. Romans 15:7–13. Who would glorify God and why? Who would they praise as ruler over the nations and why?

    c. Philippians 3:20–21. To whose kingdom do believers belong? Who is the Savior and what will he do for his people?

    d. 1 Corinthians 8:4–6. How many gods are there? Who is that God?

The Truth of the Matter
Caesar Is Not Lord!

During Paul's day, emperor worship was the fastest-growing religion in the world. The "good news" of the gospel of Imperial Rome taught that Caesar, acclaimed as the son of God, was Lord of the world—Lord, Savior, Son of God, and God! That gospel was delivered with power through military victory, and Caesar demanded allegiance from all of his subjects for bringing salvation and peace to the nations. Rejection of that gospel meant crucifixion.

That is why there was a temple to Caesar Augustus in Galilee near the intersection of the *Via Maris* and the road to Damascus and a nearly identical temple on the highest hill in Antioch of Pisidia. The Roman emperors saw an opportunity to promote their deity and thus unify a religiously and culturally diverse empire. Especially in the Roman provinces of Asia Minor, declaring the emperor's divinity became standard practice.

In contrast to the emperor's assertion that peace came through power and military victory, Paul taught that peace came by the grace of God (Romans 1:7), through Jesus' sacrifice and the selfless obedience to Christ and serving of others practiced by his disciples. This "good news" radically challenged and undermined the Imperial power of Rome and the emperor's claim to be the divine source of life.

Paul did not openly revolt against the emperor, for that would have denied the very life of Jesus whose power easily could have destroyed Caesar. However, to proclaim Jesus as the Son of God was to deny Caesar his highest honor. To confess Jesus as Lord was to commit treason. That treason eventually cost Paul his life. Paul indeed had become like his Rabbi Jesus who died, in part, because he declared the truth of a kingdom not of this world.

Reflection

Even though Paul eventually went to Rome in chains, his desire to preach God's message never waned. Within days of his arrival in Rome, Paul spoke to the leaders of the Jews as had been his custom (Acts 28:16–28). When they did not embrace his message, he began teaching the Gentiles. Imagine how thrilled he was when for two years while under house arrest in Rome—in the city of the emperor—he was able to preach the kingdom of God to everyone who came to see him (Acts 28:30–31)!

> What kind of passion and conviction led Paul, a follower of Jesus, to risk his life to teach a message that was deeply offensive to the emperor?

> What kind of commitment to obey God in all things led Paul first to *not go* to Rome and later to *go* to Rome, even though it would cost him his life?

> If God had commissioned you to teach a message that Rome considered to be treasonous, would you have wanted to go to Rome and meet Nero? Why or why not?

Memorize

The following night the Lord stood near Paul and said, "Take courage! As you have testified about me in Jerusalem, so you must also testify in Rome."

Acts 23:11

Day Three/chosen and prepared to be a Disciple

The Very Words of God

> *But the Lord said to Ananias, "Go! This man is my chosen instrument to carry my name before the Gentiles and their kings and before the people of Israel."*
>
> Acts 9:15

Bible Discovery

Who Was Paul?

Before taking the Roman name *Paul*, he was known by his Jewish name, *Saul*. Born a free Roman citizen to Jewish parents, he was unusual from birth. There is much to investigate in Saul's background that will help you to better understand this passionate Jewish follower of Jesus the Messiah.

1. Write down what the following Scripture passages reveal about young Saul so that you can begin seeing the many ways God prepared him for his future task.

   a. Acts 22:3, 25–29; 23:6

   b. 2 Corinthians 11:22

   c. Philippians 3:4–6

Did You Know?

The phrase "Hebrew of Hebrews" that Paul used to describe himself in Philippians 3:5 is a colloquial expression revealing that he was fluent in Hebrew and of Hebrew-speaking parents, an unusual background for a person born outside Israel in the Greek world.

---

2. From his earliest days, Saul was a zealous and dedicated follower of God. He studied under Gamaliel, perhaps the most highly respected rabbi of his day, which indicates that he must have been a dedicated and brilliant student of the Torah. Gamaliel was the grandson of Hillel, who founded the more lenient school of Torah and whose interpretations of Torah—such as "love your neighbor as yourself"—were often fairly close to those of Jesus. According to Jewish tradition, Gamaliel also taught Greek wisdom so his disciples could relate the Torah to Hellenistic Romans.

   a. In what ways would studying under Gamaliel have prepared Saul for his future as a disciple of Jesus long before he even met Jesus?

   b. Read Exodus 2:1–10. In what ways might Saul's training have been similar to Moses' training as Pharaoh's son prior to being given his mission from God?

3. Judging from his response to the testimony of Jesus' disciples, what kind of a student of the Torah and rabbi do you think Gamaliel was? What kind of training and preparation do you think Saul would have received from him? (See Acts 5:27–40.)

4. How did Saul treat Christians—those who belonged to "the Way"? (See Acts 9:1–2.)

5. In light of what 1 John 2:6 reveals about a disciple (a disciple passionately desires to be like his rabbi), was Saul being a "good disciple" of Gamaliel in his treatment of Christians? Why or why not?

Reflection

A disciple of a Jewish rabbi would know the Hebrew Bible. Read the following samples from Paul's writings and compare them to the Hebrew text.

- Romans 12:19 and Deuteronomy 32:35
- Romans 12:20 and Proverbs 25:21–22
- 2 Corinthians 8:15 and Exodus 16:18
- Galatians 4:27 and Isaiah 54:1

   What do these examples reveal about Paul's knowledge of the Hebrew Bible and his preparation to take the message of God's kingdom to the world?

How would he have learned the text so well?

Who else used the Hebrew text in his everyday teaching?

What does Paul's knowledge of Scripture reveal about our need to know the Bible—the very words of God?

How did God use Paul's nationality, background as a child, and study under Gamaliel to prepare him to follow Jesus? To share the gospel with others?

In what ways does this give you confidence that God has prepared you to share the message of his kingdom in your world?

Day four/Saul Becomes a Disciple of Jesus

The Very Words of God

Follow my example, as I follow the example of Christ. I praise you for remembering me in everything and for holding to the teachings, just as I passed them on to you.

1 Corinthians 11:1–2

Bible Discovery

Saul Learns the Yoke of a New Rabbi

When he met Jesus, Saul was already an accomplished rabbi who had been discipled under the great Jewish rabbi, Gamaliel. But after encountering Jesus on the Damascus road (Acts 9), Saul had to learn how his new Rabbi—Jesus—interpreted the Hebrew Bible. Eventually he became a teacher (rabbi) in his own right, but it didn't happen overnight. Consider how Saul, a passionate follower of God, humbled himself to study as a disciple again before taking on the task to which Jesus called him—that of becoming the greatest teacher to the Jews and Gentiles of the Roman world that Jesus' movement has ever known.

1. Christians today sometimes speak of Paul's "conversion" to Christianity and give the impression that he is the post-Jewish hero who left Judaism behind and formed a new faith when he met Jesus. Certainly meeting Jesus changed his life and mission, but he never stopped being Jewish. In fact, his Jewish ways—such as being a *talmid* of Jesus and worshiping in both the synagogue and the temple—became the context within which he followed Jesus the Messiah. Acts 9:1–22 and 22:1–22 provide valuable insight into ways in which Paul's encounter with Jesus did and did not change him.

    a. How did Saul's life, particularly in response to the growing Christian community, change as a result of meeting Jesus? Do you think he believed he had changed religions? Why or why not?

b. After his encounter with Jesus, where did Saul go to share his message, and why did he go there? Would he have gone there if he no longer considered himself to be Jewish? Why or why not?

c. Decades after he met Jesus on the Damascus road, how did Paul address the Jews in Jerusalem? What does this indicate about his identity as a Jew? (See Acts 22:1–5.)

Think About It!

As an accomplished student of the Hebrew Scriptures, Saul knew the details of the life stories of the Hebrew prophets—a bit like an avid sports fan today would know the statistics of his favorite player. So imagine the impact of Saul's encounter with Jesus when he realized how similar the circumstances of his calling were to the circumstances of the great heroes of the Jewish faith when God called them to serve him! Consider the similarities:

Similarity of Circumstances	Saul (Paul)	Isaiah	Jeremiah	Ezekiel
Set apart from birth	✓	✓	✓	
Heard the Lord speaking	✓	✓	✓	✓
Saw a light	✓			✓

Fell down	✓			✓
Was told to stand on his feet	✓			✓
Given a mission to speak to the Gentiles and/or Jews	✓	✓	✓	✓

No wonder Saul was so passionate about taking the message of God's kingdom to everyone!

(See Isaiah 49:1–6; Jeremiah 1:4–10; Ezekiel 1:4–5, 25–2:3; Acts 9:3–6, 15; Galatians 1:13–16.)

2. Read Acts 9:26–28 and then answer the following questions.

    a. When Saul first traveled to Jerusalem after he met Jesus, who did he want to meet?

    b. What problem did Saul encounter with the believers in Jerusalem, and who took responsibility for him and may have helped him grow as a disciple of Jesus?

    c. What at least suggests that this became a discipling relationship? (See also Acts 11:22–26.)

Did You Know?

During New Testament times, every Jewish rabbi invited his disciples to take his "yoke of the Torah," meaning to shoulder the responsibility of obedience to the Torah—God's Word—as that rabbi interpreted it. Though there were many rabbis, each one followed one of two basic schools of thought—Hillel or Shammai. Nonetheless, differences occurred between the yokes of the rabbis. When Saul chose Jesus the Messiah as his Rabbi, he had to learn to reinterpret the Hebrew Bible in light of Jesus' actions and teaching rather than those of his former rabbi Gamaliel (Hillel's grandson). That took considerable time. Yet because Jesus' teaching and Scripture interpretations in many respects were similar to those of the school of Hillel, Saul had a huge advantage.

3. Several years after he began following Jesus, Saul again went to Jerusalem. With whom did he stay and why was that visit significant? (See Galatians 1:18–19.)

4. Years later, who besides Barnabas and Titus encouraged and assisted Saul in his ministry? How did Saul view himself as a disciple of Jesus? How did the leaders of the church in Jerusalem view him? In what ways did Saul's calling differ from theirs? (See Galatians 2:1–2, 8–10.)

Reflection

In the Jewish culture, when more than one name is written, the most important person's name is usually listed first. It is intriguing that until Paul first spoke in the synagogue of Antioch (see Acts 13:16–41), Barnabas usually is listed before Saul/Paul (Acts 11:25–26, 30; 12:25; 13:1–2, 7). From then on, with few exceptions (Acts 14:14; 15:12, 25), Paul is mentioned before Barnabas (Acts 13:42–43, 46, 50; 14:1, 3, 20, 23; 15:2, 22, 35–36).

> What indications does Scripture give that Barnabas functioned as Saul's second rabbi (teacher) until Paul became a disciple who was ready to proclaim the full message of Jesus?

> How might Paul's walk with Jesus have been different if believers had not "taken him under their wings" and taught him about being a disciple of Jesus?

> As time passed, how did Paul become more and more like Jesus?

> How might your walk with Jesus be different if you were to imitate Paul as he imitated Jesus?

> Which person(s) might God want you to disciple, and what would be involved in doing that?

Day Five/God's plan for the god fearers

The Very Words of God

God, who knows the heart, showed that he accepted them [Gentile believers] by giving the Holy Spirit to them, just as he did to us. He made no distinction between us and them, for he purified their hearts by faith. Now then, why do you try to test God by putting on the necks of the disciples a yoke that neither we nor our fathers have been able to bear? No! We believe it is through the grace of our Lord Jesus that we are saved, just as they are.

Acts 15:8–11

Bible Discovery

God Never Forgot the Gentiles

God drew many pagan people to himself long before the message of Jesus came to the Roman world. Attracted to the God of Israel by the witness and lifestyle of faithful Jews, God-fearing Gentiles left their gods and associated with the synagogue communities. Although these Gentiles lacked experience in how to obey God, they loved and worshiped the God of the Hebrew Bible. Some of them converted completely to Judaism while others committed themselves to obey the Torah and participate as much as possible in the community of his people. When God brought to fruition the gospel of Jesus as Messiah, many God-fearers accepted the Jewish Rabbi as God's Son and their Savior. The Bible exploration below will help you understand God's plan and hope for the Gentiles from the time he called Abraham.

1. According to Genesis 12:1–3, what was God's purpose for calling Abraham to follow him?

2. How were the Israelites to treat their Gentile (alien) neighbors and why? How might this relate to God's purpose for Israel to be a blessing to the world? (See Exodus 20:10; 22:21; Deuteronomy 10:17–19; 24:14, 17–21; 26:12.)

3. Who were to be God's witnesses, and were they effective? (See Isaiah 43:1, 10–12.)

4. What did the prophets say would happen concerning the pagans who lived around Israel? (See Isaiah 66:18–20; Micah 4:1–3; Zechariah 8:23.)

5. What part were Jesus' followers to have in completing God's command to be his witnesses to the ends of the earth? (See Acts 1:1–8.)

6. Read Isaiah 56:3–8 and then answer the following questions.

   a. What has God promised to do for Gentiles who faithfully worship him?

   b. Has God limited faith in the God of the Hebrew Bible to the Jews? Why or why not?

7. Why do you think God's full acceptance and blessing of God-fearing Gentiles was difficult for some Jews to accept? Is this why Paul's teaching that Gentiles were included in God's plan of salvation angered some of the Jews in Antioch?

For Greater Understanding ...
What to Do with the God-Fearers?

Apparently the Jews debated about how to deal with the God-fearers who aligned themselves with the God of the Jews. There was no question that some of the Levitical laws made it difficult for Gentiles to become fully Jewish. Circumcision (Genesis 17:11), eating kosher (Leviticus 11), turning away from idolatry (Exodus 20:3–4), and wearing special clothing such as tassels (Numbers 15:37–40) were moderate to very difficult practices for those who had been immersed in the pagan culture of the Roman Empire. So, should the Jewish community require the God-fearers to convert, be circumcised, and become Jewish in every way? Or, would it be acceptable for the God-fearers simply to renounce their pagan practices and follow the morality of the Jewish community without taking on such responsibilities as circumcision and wearing of tassels? The Jewish community was not in agreement on how to resolve this issue.

This problem followed Gentiles into the community of Jesus, and Acts 15:1–31 describes how the Jerusalem Council resolved this issue. The apostles and elders discussed the nature of salvation, the position of the Gentiles before God, and the meaning of obedience to the Torah. They concluded that God-fearers could accept the basic requirements (sometimes called the laws of Noah) such as abstaining from food sacrificed to idols, from blood, from meat of strangled animals, and from sexual immorality, but did not have to keep all the practices of the Torah.

Reflection

The centurion who built the synagogue in Capernaum and whose servant Jesus healed was apparently a God-fearer (Luke 7:1–10). Even more striking is Cornelius the centurion, who is actually called a God-fearer in the text. Read his story in Acts 10:1–48, and write down all that God did in and through the life of this one God-fearing Gentile.

> In what ways did Cornelius witness for God before he became a believer?

> How much influence for God did Cornelius have on his family and local community?

> How did God use Cornelius to teach Peter, a bold disciple of Jesus?

> In what way(s) did God prepare people—Jew and Gentile—to receive Jesus and his message?

> God has prepared people of all nations and languages to hear his message and become his disciples. How might he be using you to prepare people to receive or to teach this same message today?

Memorize

*And foreigners who bind themselves to the LORD, to serve him, to love
the name of the LORD, and to worship him, all who keep the Sabbath
without desecrating it and who hold fast to my covenant—these I will
bring to my holy mountain and give them joy in my house of prayer.
Their burnt offerings and sacrifices will be accepted on my altar; for
my house will be called a house of prayer for all nations.*

Isaiah 56:6–7

An unlikely Disciple

Many who have followed God through the ages have experienced how he used them in ways they did not expect. Consider, for example, Moses who fled Egypt never expecting to see Pharaoh's courts again. What about Ruth, the Moabite woman who was brought into the lineage of Jesus? And what about the young fishermen of Galilee who apparently didn't quite make the grade as star students but were chosen by Jesus to be his *talmidim*? Who would ever have expected that? And of course there was Saul, the zealous (or was it overzealous?) Pharisee who became a disciple of Jesus, the very one he persecuted.

But unlikely disciples don't become great champions of the faith overnight. They must be trained to passionately and faithfully obey God. They must, in New Testament language, learn to walk as Jesus walked. They must, as Jesus commanded in Matthew 28:19–20, become disciples who make disciples. In this session we'll see how Paul learns to make disciples as Jesus commanded.

We'll begin with Paul's first teaching tour, when he traveled quickly from place to place faithfully preaching the message God had given to him. Many Jews and Gentiles came to believe in Jesus and a number of churches were formed. For some reason, however, Paul—a Jewish rabbi who had studied under the brilliant rabbi Gamaliel—does not appear to be "making disciples" in the Jewish sense. We don't, for example, read about believers who lived with Paul in order to become like him (and therefore like Jesus) in their walk with God. This is surprising because Paul, of all people, knew firsthand how time-consuming it is to be a disciple. He had dedicated decades of his life to being a disciple—first of Gamaliel, then of Jesus.

Partway through his second teaching tour, Paul begins changing his missions strategy. In rural Lystra, he chose the young man who appears to be his first disciple—Timothy—just as Jesus chose his twelve disciples in rural Galilee. Then, when Paul reaches Corinth, Paul continues to walk with Jesus by making disciples. He stayed nearly two years in Corinth during the last half of his second tour, then spent most of his third teaching tour (nearly three years) in Ephesus. During this time, disciples accompanied him every day listening to him teach and imitating his every step so they could learn to walk as Jesus walked.

As we consider Paul's walk with Jesus, we'll see that Timothy was an unlikely choice for a disciple, just as each of the disciples whom Jesus chose were unlikely choices. An outsider to the Jewish community through no fault of his own, Timothy stands as an example of how God often unfolds awesome plans through unlikely disciples who are fully committed to him and seek to walk as Jesus walked (1 John 2:6).

Can we identify with Timothy? Sure! We easily underestimate God's ability to use us, but there's great news! Just as God had great plans for Timothy, he has great plans for each of us. As we are faithful in walking as Jesus walked, God will use us in ways we do not expect or deserve.

opening Thoughts (3 minutes)

The Very Words of God

It has always been my ambition to preach the gospel where Christ was not known.

Romans 15:20

Think About It

Think for a moment about the people—from the Scriptures, from more recent history, from your life—whom God has used to accomplish amazing things for him. Which ones, at least at first, seemed to be unfit for the task? What does this suggest about the kinds of people God delights to use in mighty ways?

DVD Notes (29 minutes)

Why Galatia?

Teachings from a sheep pen

Lystra

The myth

The miracles

The *mamzer*

DVD Highlights (4 minutes)

1. What are your impressions of Galatia—its terrain, beauty, isolation, and people (or lack thereof!)?

   Is it what you expected it to be? Why or why not?

2. In what ways do these images of Galatia affect your impression and understanding of Paul and his passion for teaching the gospel message to those who had not heard it?

3. When you consider how much time Paul spent walking through this part of his world, what do you learn about his commitment to obey Jesus and walk as Jesus walked?

   Do you think Paul ever struggled with why the path God led him on required so much time in the "wilderness" of Galatia? Explain your answer.

small group Bible Discovery and group Discussion (13 minutes)

Why Galatia?

During his three teaching tours, Paul walked through Galatia four times—probably logging more than a thousand miles! Imagine him teaching the message of Jesus in cities, towns, villages, and in conversations with shepherds, farmers, and other people he might meet along the way. Let's see what Scripture suggests about why Paul was so determined to minister as he did in Galatia.

Overview of Paul's Teaching Tours in Galatia

First Tour (Acts 13 – 14) c. AD 46 – 48

After teaching in Cyprus, Barnabas and Paul went to Antioch of Pisidia via Perga. Fleeing opposition in Antioch, they went through Galatia to Iconium and Lystra. Opposition from Antioch followed them in each of these cities, so they went to Derbe, where they continued teaching. Weeks later, they retraced their steps through Galatia, encouraging the believers in every city they previously had visited. Then they returned to Jerusalem.

Second Tour (Acts 16 – 18:22) c. AD 49 – 51

After parting company with Barnabas and John Mark, Paul and Silas walked through Galatia from the east, strengthening new churches as they went. Among the places they stopped were Derbe, Iconium, and Lystra where Paul chose Timothy to become his disciple. They then continued on to Macedonia (Greece) and later returned to Antioch (Syria) by sea with a brief stop in Ephesus.

Third Tour (Acts 18:23 – 21:15) c. AD 52 – 56

Paul walked from place to place throughout Galatia strengthening believers. He then took the interior road to Ephesus and after a stay there continued to Macedonia where he also encouraged the disciples. He then headed back by sea for what would be his final return to Jerusalem.

1. On several occasions during their first teaching tour, Paul and Barnabas faced great opposition as they preached the good news of Jesus in Galatia. Notice the kind of opposition they faced and how they responded to it.

Scripture	Location	Type of Opposition	Their Response
Acts 13:49–51			
Acts 14:1–7			
Acts 14:8, 19–22			

2. What motivated and empowered Paul and Barnabas to continue teaching the message of Jesus wherever they traveled, even when they faced great suffering? (See Romans 15:20–21.)

3. The Bible doesn't tell us exactly why Paul went to Galatia or why he went through the region so many times when he could have taken alternate routes to his later destinations. However, the record of Paul's second teaching tour gives us significant insight into how he decided where to teach. Read Acts 16:6–10 and discuss its significance in light of what you already know about Paul's mission, message, and passionate commitment to follow

God. Do you think Paul always felt that God directed him during his teaching tours? Explain your answer.

4. Houses in the small villages of what was once known as Galatia are remarkably similar to those of Paul's time. Homes are built of mud brick or small stones with flat, clay roofs. They often have a garden with a canopy for grape vines under which families sit during the heat of the day or the evening.

Tiered grape arbors in the village of Kyali look similar to the grape arbors written about in the Scriptures.

Read 1 Kings 4:25 and Micah 4:2 – 5 and consider how, in true rabbinic tradition, scenes such as these would have provided Paul with a theme for communicating the message of Jesus.

Profile of Galatia

Galatia is a beautiful, rugged, and fertile agricultural region among the Taurus Mountains in central Asia Minor (Turkey today). The area is isolated geographically and to this day has few large towns or cities. Most of its people were (and are) rural farmers who lived in widely separated villages. Although a major trade route between Persia and the West, the *Via Sebaste*, went through the region, most of the people remained independent of Roman influence and the Hellenistic culture of larger cities such as Ephesus.

Mountains, farmland, and pastureland characterize the landscape of Galatia.

Galatia was settled by fiercely independent, warlike raiders who came from Gaul, the region of western Europe that we know of as France, Belgium, and Germany. In about 240 BC, the king of Pergamum, Attalus I, defeated the Galatians, but they were never greatly influenced by the Greeks. When Roman influence arrived, the Galatians were known as fierce fighters and were prized as mercenaries.

Galatia became a Roman province during the reign of Caesar Augustus (about 2 BC), who tried to Romanize it by populating thirteen Roman colonies with veterans of the best Roman legions (fifth and seventh). Three of these colonies—Antioch of Pisidia, Iconium, and Lystra—were locations where Paul taught during his first tour. Each of these cities also had a significant population of Jews who were forcibly moved into the area about 250 years before Paul arrived. Paul came back to this region on each of his teaching tours and addressed the book of Galatians to churches established there.

Faith Lesson (4 minutes)

1. Read Ephesians 6:19–20. Which words or phrases stand out to you? Why? What do they reveal about Paul's passionate commitment to God and people who had not heard the gospel?

2. How courageous was Paul in his attempts to preach the gospel where it was not known? Which examples of his faith and bold courage mean the most to you?

3. If you knew that you could play a pivotal and influential role in guiding someone to Jesus, how would you live your life differently? What would you be willing to do or sacrifice to enable that to happen?

closing (1 minute)

Read the following verse aloud. Then pray, asking God to give you a passionate commitment and bold courage so that you will be as ready and eager to follow God's calling as Paul was.

Memorize

Pray also for me, that whenever I open my mouth, words may be given me so that I will fearlessly make known the mystery of the gospel, for which I am an ambassador in chains. Pray that I may declare it fearlessly, as I should.

Ephesians 6:19–20

walk as jesus walked

In-Depth Personal Study Sessions

day one/paul becomes more like jesus

The Very Words of God

I am not ashamed of the gospel, because it is the power of God for the salvation of everyone who believes: first for the Jew, then for the Gentile.

Romans 1:16

Bible Discovery

Paul Matures as a Disciple

There's no doubt that Paul was a faithful disciple of God. Much of the New Testament testifies of how God used Paul to bring Jesus' message to the world. Yet in our desire to honor Paul, we may forget that he also had to learn to follow and obey the Lord just as Moses, David, Peter, and many others had learned (sometimes through bitter experiences). Don't forget that Paul began persecuting believers because he was passionately devoted to God and his Word! However, having misunderstood that Word and having persecuted Jesus and his followers, Paul had to relearn how to submit to God's ways and interpret the Hebrew Bible as Jesus, his new Rabbi, interpreted it. Let's see how Scripture shows Paul learning to become like Jesus as he walked through Galatia.

Did You Know?

During Paul's first teaching tour, he traveled only with Barnabas. Some scholars believe that Barnabas was a rabbi to Paul during this time, so it is likely that as they walked Barnabas

---

taught Paul how to reinterpret the Hebrew Bible in light of Jesus. The isolation of their path gave them many opportunities to recite the Hebrew text, discuss issues, consider how people had responded to their message, and develop new illustrations for their teaching. Their conversations may have been much like the interaction between Jesus and his disciples as the disciples walked with their Rabbi from place to place.

Paul and Barnabas walked on roads through the Galatian countryside that would have been very similar to this one (top). Notice how much this area of Galatia looks like the road from Chorazin to Capernaum (bottom), a route Jesus and his disciples frequently walked.

1. The apostle Paul was always zealous and bold in his walk with God. This doesn't mean that his actions were always perfectly in line with what God desired.

    a. How do we know Paul knew he had to learn some things along the way? (See 1 Timothy 1:15–16.)

    b. What did Paul and Barnabas say to jealous Jews in Antioch? (See Acts 13:44–46.)

    c. In light of that bold condemnation, what's significant about where Paul and Barnabas first spoke in Iconium? (See Acts 14:1.)

    d. What truth about God's message may Paul and Barnabas have considered on the journey from Antioch of Pisidia to Iconium that led them to begin teaching in the synagogue of Iconium? (See Romans 1:16.)

2. Read the story of Paul and Barnabas in Iconium in Acts 14:1–7.

    a. What situation resulted from their teaching in Iconium?

b. Why might God have intervened miraculously in this way, at this time?

c. In what ways is the situation Paul and Barnabas faced in Iconium similar to situations Jesus faced during his ministry? (See Mark 3:1–8; Luke 19:47–48.)

3. Paul had one consuming passion throughout his ministry. What was it, and how might it explain why, early in his ministry, he visited so many places but never stayed in each place for very long? (See Acts 26:15–18; Romans 15:18–21.)

4. What other factors may have affected the length of Paul's visits during his first and part of his second teaching tours?

a. See Acts 14:5, 19–20; 16:19–24.

b. See 1 Corinthians 7:29–31; 1 Thessalonians 4:15–18.

Data File
What Is a Disciple?

The word *disciple* in the New Testament refers to two types of believers:

- Any believer in Jesus (Acts 6:7; 11:26). This more Greek-like use of *disciple* generically refers to a believer who desires to know more.
- The Hebrew use of *disciple* (*talmid*) is more stringent and refers to disciples who passionately desire to learn to follow God by observing and imitating their rabbi's example (Mark 3:14).

Jesus desires that all believers (disciples) become disciples (*talmidim* like Jesus' twelve disciples who imitated him) and then make disciples.

5. When Paul arrived in Corinth partway through his second teaching tour, a dramatic change took place in his ministry. See Acts 18:9 – 11.

   a. What happened to Paul that had never before happened during one of his teaching tours?

   b. Although we don't have enough information to draw firm conclusions, what insight does this give you into why Paul may have conducted his early ministry as he did?

c. What did the situation God had prepared in Corinth allow Paul to do that he had not been able to do previously? In what ways did this enable Paul to enter into a new phase of learning to walk as Jesus walked?

Reflection

Write down the evidence you see of Paul's passion for God and his commitment to share the gospel message as Jesus commanded him to do.

Did Paul follow Jesus any more or less intensely before or after Corinth? What about his ministry was different, what was the same? (See Acts 18:18–23.)

What does this tell you about how we learn to live for Jesus in whatever circumstances we find ourselves? What example did Paul and Barnabas set for us by their commitment to preach God's message wherever they went, even when they faced great opposition, even when they did not understand why God had placed them where they were?

Pray about how you could become more like Paul, a disciple who was intent on walking as Jesus walked and had an intense desire to share Jesus and a willingness to follow God's leading.

Day Two/Teaching God's Message in a New Way

The Very Words of God

Men, why are you doing this? We too are only men, human like you. We are bringing you good news, telling you to turn from these worthless things to the living God, who made heaven and earth and sea and everything in them.

Acts 14:15

Bible Discovery

Paul Speaks through the Culture of His Hearers

It isn't difficult to understand why Paul wanted to teach in Antioch of Pisidia, a large city nestled in the foothills of the remote and sparsely populated Galatian countryside. By taking God's message to Antioch, Paul could reach the most influential Jews and Gentiles of Galatia. Due to the city's strong ties with Rome, Paul may have thought that a message taught in Antioch would not only reach a region where the gospel message was unknown, but could have a far-reaching impact on the Roman Empire. Iconium was also a significant Galatian city with a strong Jewish population, so it made sense for Paul to teach there. But why did Paul go to Lystra, an out-of-the-way town with fewer than a thousand people? What new experiences and special purpose(s) did God have in mind for Paul in Lystra? Let's consider what the Scriptures say about Paul's activities there.

1. As Paul grew in his walk with Jesus and his understanding of the Hebrew Scriptures in light of Jesus, he made powerful connections with a variety of audiences that had never heard of

Jesus. Two of his teaching experiences in Galatia—Antioch and Lystra—are examples of how he effectively communicated the gospel message to diverse audiences. First, review Paul's teaching in Antioch (see Acts 13:16–41), taking note of the following details:

a. Where and to whom did Paul speak?

b. On what did he base his message? To what extent would his audience have known and believed what he was saying?

c. Through what context did Paul weave in the news of Jesus? In what ways would this have helped his audience understand his message?

d. What is the evidence that the people heard and understood Paul's message, regardless of whether or not they agreed with it? (See Acts 13:42–52.)

Profile of Lystra

Located in Galatia, Lystra was about 600 miles by road from Jerusalem, 320 miles from Ephesus, 30 miles south of Iconium, and more than 110 miles from Antioch of Pisidia. The *tel* of Lystra (an unexcavated mound about five acres in size that is composed of ruins of various settlements) was first identified in 1885 by an inscription on a stone found in a farmer's field at the base of the tel.

When Caesar Augustus attempted to Romanize Galatia around 25 BC, Lystra was established as the southernmost of thirteen colonies of veteran Roman legionnaires. It provided important protection against invasion of Roman areas in the north, but the area was never brought fully under Roman control. When Paul visited Lystra, the thousand or so residents still spoke their ancient Lycaonian language, and the city was more like a frontier town than a Roman city.

In addition to Roman legionnaires and native Lycaonians, Lystra apparently had a Jewish community although there are no known records of a synagogue and no excavation of the tel has been done. Despite the mixed response to Paul's first visit, early church records reveal that Lystra had its own bishop for five hundred years after Paul's teaching tours, so God clearly blessed Paul's ministry.

Today the tel of ancient Lystra is surrounded by farmland and linden trees.

2. Now read Acts 14:8–18, where Paul spoke in Lystra to a very different audience, and answer the following questions:

   a. Generally, in what type of a place does it appear Paul spoke?

   b. As he spoke (and Scripture doesn't tell us what he said), what did Paul notice about one of his listeners, and what did Paul do in response?

   c. Miraculous healing usually communicates that supernatural power is at work. Did the people of Lystra get that message? How hard did Paul have to work to convince them it was *God's* divine power at work? To what extent was he successful?

   d. Judging from their response to God healing the crippled man through Paul, what were the spiritual beliefs of the people of Lystra? Do you think they were devout in their religious practices? Why or why not?

   e. What kinds of things did Paul say to the people of Lystra in order to present God's message in the context of (and in contrast to) their spiritual beliefs? (Go ahead and make a list of them!)

     f.   To what extent did Paul refer to the Hebrew Scriptures and Jesus as he told the people of Lystra who God was and what he had done for them? Why do you think he chose this method? Do you think this was a compromise of the message God had given him?

3. What do you think Paul's purpose was in emphasizing the Hebrew Scriptures during his teaching in Antioch but taking a different approach in Lystra during his first visit there?

Think About It!

The people of Lystra believed that Zeus, king of the gods, provided rain and crops. Hermes was a son of Zeus. He was the god of shepherds and the messenger of the gods. Reread Acts 14:15–17 with these facts in mind and think about what you would have understood Paul to be saying if you had been a resident of Lystra.

4. All religious Jews believed that the greatest commandment was to love God with all one's heart, soul, and strength (Deuteronomy 6:5), so imagine how Paul—a devout Pharisee and faithful disciple of Jesus who was passionately committed to obeying God in everything—felt when the residents of Lystra wanted to worship *him* as God! (See Acts 14:11–18.)

a. When Paul and Barnabas learned that the people of Lystra wanted to offer sacrifices to them, how did they respond? Do you think their actions got the attention of the people? What was the result?

b. In what ways would the images and words Paul and Barnabas used to explain who God is and what he had done connect with the life experiences of the people of Lystra?

5. Read Acts 14:19–20 and then answer the following questions.

a. What happened to Paul in Lystra soon after he finished talking about the living God?

b. After this, what did Paul do? What do you think this action communicated to the people of Lystra?

6. How do we know that Paul's efforts in Lystra bore spiritual fruit? (See Acts 14:20–23; 16:1–3.)

Reflection

Review Paul's messages in Antioch and Lystra and consider what Paul did to communicate God's truth in ways people understood—whether or not they agreed with him.

What do you learn from Paul's example that will help you communicate God's message to people in your world?

What do you learn about God's willingness to create opportunities for us to share his truth in the "language" of people we encounter?

How did Paul respond to the Lycaonians after they stoned him, and what did this reveal about his passion for God and for carrying out the mission God had given him?

Early church records reveal that Lystra had its own bishop for five hundred years after Paul's teaching tours! So although Paul probably saw little spiritual fruit of his teaching in Lystra, God clearly blessed his ministry there. How willing are you to passionately live out and share the message of Jesus in your spheres of influence even when you don't see the results you would like?

Data File
Stoning

Stoning was an accepted method of capital punishment in the ancient world. Through Moses, God prescribed how stoning was to be used in Israel. A person could be stoned for offenses such as sacrificing a child to Molech, being a medium or spiritist, blaspheming the Lord, breaking Sabbath rules, trying to turn another person away from God, violating covenant with God by worshiping other gods, being a false prophet, or being promiscuous. (See Leviticus 20:2, 27; 24:16; Numbers 15:32–36; Deuteronomy 13:6–11; 17:2–6; 18:18–21; 22:20–24.)

Rules for stoning were codified and written about a century after the Lycaonians stoned Paul, but the following basic rules were probably already in place.

- The accused person would be brought to a place more than twice the height of a man (usually twelve to fifteen feet).
- The accused person would be given a chance to confess and receive God's forgiveness before being stoned.
- The accused person would be bound and pushed off the high place by the two accusing witnesses. (According to Deuteronomy 17:7, "The hands of the witnesses must be the first in putting him to death, and then the hands of all the people.")
- Then, each person who believed the accused person was guilty would throw one stone of any size onto the accused until all had participated. The fate of the accused person—whether life or death—was then left in the hands of God.

Memorize

I have become all things to all men so that by all possible means I might save some.

1 Corinthians 9:22

Day Three/Paul chooses a Disciple

The Very Words of God

Follow my example, as I follow the example of Christ.

1 Corinthians 11:1

Bible Discovery

Paul Chooses Timothy

During his second teaching tour, Paul and Silas left Antioch (Syria) and began encouraging the disciples in the churches of Syria and Cilicia. They then visited the churches Paul and Barnabas had established in Galatia during their first teaching tour. While in Lystra, Paul met a young disciple named Timothy, and from that point on Paul and Timothy's lives were knit together in the ministry of the gospel. So who was Timothy, and why was his relationship with Paul so significant to both of them?

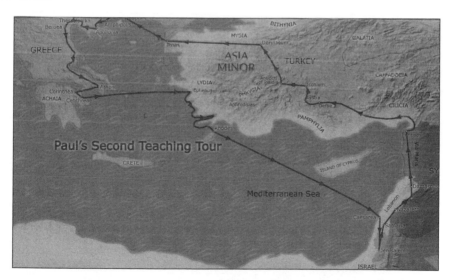

Paul's second teaching tour

1. Read Acts 16:1 – 2; 1 Timothy 4:12; and 2 Timothy 1:5 – 7; 3:14 – 15. Based on these passages, construct as complete a personal history and spiritual character profile of Timothy as you can. As you continue your study, these details about Timothy will become more significant to you.

2. Although Scripture does not record Paul specifically calling Timothy a disciple (*talmid*), Scripture indicates that they traveled and ministered together for years and records many instances of Paul teaching, training, and being an example of Jesus to Timothy.

    a. Where do we know Timothy and Paul ministered together? As you read these passages, what indications do you see that Timothy was following Paul as a disciple would?

Scripture Passage	Paul and Timothy's Ministry Locations and Relationship
Acts 20:1 – 4	
2 Cor. 1:1	
Acts 18:1, 5; 1 Thess. 1:1; 2 Thess. 1:1	
Phili. 1:1, 12 – 14; 2:22; Col. 1:1; Philem. 1	

    b. During the first and second centuries, a disciple was always with his teacher (rabbi) and called him "father"; the rabbi called his disciple "child," "son," or "brother." What language does Paul use in the following verses that would indicate he thought of Timothy as his disciple? (See 2 Corinthians 1:1; Philippians 1:1; Colossians 1:1; 1 Timothy 1:2; 2 Timothy 1:2.)

c. What in the following passages indicates that Paul and Timothy had a rabbi/disciple relationship? What similarities do you see to the relationship Jesus had with his disciples? (See Acts 20:1–4; Philippians 2:22; 1 Thessalonians 3:2.)

d. In what ways do you see Timothy growing spiritually through his association with Paul? How is Timothy's growth similar to the way in which the disciples grew as they followed Jesus? (See 2 Corinthians 1:19; 2 Timothy 1:1–5; 3:10–14.)

e. Which traits of a passionate disciple did Paul encourage in Timothy? Was Paul a good example of these? (See 1 Timothy 4:11–14; 6:11; 2 Timothy 1:6; 3:14–17.)

Reflection

Read 1 Timothy 1:1–6, 15–19 and note where Paul assigned Timothy to serve as "pastor" (rabbi). What is significant about this location and the great responsibility Paul placed on Timothy? Do you think Timothy had learned to be a disciple who could make disciples? Why or why not?

In what ways did Paul encourage Timothy in this work? In what ways was Timothy still Paul's disciple?

Are you a disciple who could shoulder the spiritual responsibilities Timothy was given? What would be required for you to be such a disciple? Are you willing to commit as much of yourself to learning to walk as Jesus walked as Timothy did? Why or why not? What are the consequences of your answer?

Memorize

Don't let anyone look down on you because you are young, but set an example for the believers in speech, in life, in love, in faith, and in purity ... devote yourself to the public reading of Scripture, to preaching and to teaching.

1 Timothy 4:12–13

Day Four/Paul Makes Disciples

The Very Words of God

I no longer call you servants, because a servant does not know his master's business. Instead, I have called you friends, for everything that I have learned from my Father I have made known to you. You did not choose me, but I chose you and appointed you to go and bear fruit—fruit that will last.

John 15:15–16

Bible Discovery

After completing his first and part of his second teaching tour, Paul changed the way he went about his ministry. He chose Timothy to accompany him and was like a rabbi to Timothy as he trained him in the faith and set an example for him to follow. When Paul arrived in Corinth, he suddenly stopped moving quickly from place to place. In fact, he stayed in Corinth for a year and a half and apparently began sharing his life with several additional disciples. Consider how Paul continued growing in his walk with Jesus as he made these changes.

1. Just as Lystra marked a turning point in Paul's ministry, Corinth marked a turning point as well. Read Acts 18:1 – 11 and consider the events that happened there.

    a. Who did Paul stay with in Corinth and why? Do you think Paul was making disciples at this point? Why or why not? (verses 1 – 3)

    b. What role do you think Timothy and Silas played in Paul's ministry? (verse 5)

    c. In what ways was Paul's ministry in Corinth just as it had always been? Who did he speak to first, where, and why? What change did he make when great opposition arose? (verses 4 – 8)

d. What did God enable Paul to do in Corinth that had not been possible anywhere else? What insight does this give you into why making disciples as Jesus made disciples had not been Paul's emphasis prior to this time? (verses 9–11)

2. Just as Timothy was linked with Paul's life and ministry from the time they met, Aquila and Priscilla had a long-term connection with Paul as well.

a. What kind of relationship does it appear Paul developed with Aquila and Priscilla? Remember, he had spent a year and a half with them! (See Acts 18:18–21.)

b. Do you think Aquila and Priscilla were part of the reason Paul felt he could leave Ephesus even when the Jews asked him to stay longer? Why or why not?

c. What indicates that Aquila and Priscilla continued to make disciples as Paul had apparently taught them? (See Acts 18:24–28; Romans 16:3–5; 1 Corinthians 16:19.)

3. While on his third teaching tour, Paul took another step toward making disciples as Jesus did. Read Acts 19:1–10 and answer the following questions.

a. Who did Paul meet in Ephesus?

b. Whose disciples were they?

c. What was their response to the news of Jesus? In what ways was their response like that of Paul when he met Jesus? (See Acts 9:17–20; 19:4–9.)

d. Paul now had twelve disciples (Acts 19:7). How do you think they learned the yoke—the interpretations of the Hebrew text—of their new rabbi? Was Paul now making disciples as Jesus had done? Why or why not? (See Acts 19:8–10.)

4. How did the communities of Jesus, started through Paul's ministry, learn to be like Jesus? (See 1 Corinthians 4:16–17; 11:1–2; 1 Thessalonians 1:4–7; 1 Timothy 4:12.)

5. Why did Paul want the followers of Jesus to follow his example? Who did he want them to become like? (See 1 Corinthians 1:11 – 13; Hebrews 13:7 – 8.)

The Language and Heart of a Rabbi

Notice the close, familial, rabbi-like language Paul used in writing to his "disciples" in the cities he visited on his teaching tours.

Paul's Writings	Paul's Language
1 Corinthians 4:14 – 17; 1 Thessalonians 2:11	my dear children; father; imitate me
Philippians 2:22	as a son with his father
1 Timothy 1:18; Philemon 10	my son
Titus 1:4	my true son in our common faith
1 Corinthians 11:1 – 2; Philippians 3:17	follow my example; holding to the teachings, just as I passed them on to you; brothers
1 Thessalonians 1:4 – 6	imitators of us
1 Corinthians 7:7	wish all men were as I am
Philippians 4:9	whatever you have learned or received or heard from me, or seen in me — put it into practice
2 Timothy 1:13	what you heard from me, keep as the pattern of sound teaching

Reflection

Paul had always wanted to go to Rome to testify of Jesus. Finally, in Acts 23:11, Jesus told him that the time had come to go to Rome. Consider how Paul had fulfilled the mandate Jesus gave him (Acts 9:15). Consider all that had happened on his teaching tours and the number of disciples he had left behind. Then read Acts 20:17–31.

> Had Paul proven himself to be an obedient disciple? Had he made other obedient disciples who would carry on the work God had given him?

> Is it any less important today for believers to walk with Jesus, to imitate him in every way, and to make disciples?

Spend time in prayer, asking God to lead you into deeper discipleship. Ask him to help you learn to teach others to follow Jesus by imitating you as you walk with him. Think of at least one person whom you can show how to imitate Jesus—a child, sibling, grandchild, student, friend, coworker. We must fulfill the mandate Jesus has given us. We must become disciple makers!

Memorize

I praise you for remembering me in everything and for holding to the teachings, just as I passed them on to you.

1 Corinthians 11:2

Day Five/Paul Chooses a Mamzer

The Very Words of God

To Timothy my true son in the faith.

1 Timothy 1:2

Bible Discovery

The Most Unlikely Disciple

In some ways, Timothy was the most unlikely young man for Paul to choose as a disciple and colleague in ministry. Just consider some of the contrasts between them. Paul was a Pharisee, the son of a Pharisee. He was recognized as an outstanding student of one of the greatest rabbis, and he demonstrated remarkable passion and zeal for God. Timothy, on the other hand, was a nobody who grew up in a small town in a pagan wilderness. He was an outsider, an uncircumcised *mamzer*, who was probably unable to participate in Jewish community life at any level. Yet Timothy was the young man Paul chose as his disciple.

1. What did God command regarding the children of a forbidden marriage? (See Deuteronomy 23:2.)

2. What do we know about Timothy's family? (See Acts 16:1 – 3.)

NOTE: When Scripture refers to someone as "a Greek" rather than "a God-fearing Greek" it is a strong indication that the person is a nonbeliever. The reference to the faith of Timothy's mother further supports the idea that his father was not a follower of the God of the Bible.

3. What impact did the relationship between Timothy's mother and father have on Timothy within the Jewish community? Was it his fault?

Data File
The Mamzer

During Paul's time, Jewish communities had not settled the issue of the *mamzer* ("misbegotten" child of a forbidden marriage). However, based on the codifying of Deuteronomy 23:2 that occurred later, many of the following prohibitions were probably widely practiced.

- A *mamzer* was anyone born of a forbidden sexual relationship (incest, out of wedlock, outside a parent's marriage relationship, or a parent's marriage to or relationship with a pagan).
- Parents of a *mamzer* should not marry each other; two *mamzers* (*mamzerim*) could marry, but their offspring would be *mamzers*.
- The *mamzer* could not enter the "assembly of the LORD" (Deuteronomy 23:2), which likely prohibited community worship (in synagogue or the temple in Jerusalem), participation in communal activities such as Jewish festivals, and study with Jewish teachers.

Thus the *mamzer*, who was not hated or shunned, remained an outsider due to the sin of the parents.

---

4. Paul must have had a reason for choosing Timothy, a *mamzer*, as a disciple. Read Acts 16:1–2 and 2 Timothy 1:5; 3:14–15 and see what you learn about this unlikely, but remarkable young disciple.

a. What surprising information do we know about Timothy that may have caught Paul's attention? How hard do you think it was for a *mamzer* to learn the Hebrew Scriptures?

b. Do you think it is possible that Paul saw in Timothy a passion for God? Why or why not?

5. What do you think was the significance of Paul circumcising Timothy before they began teaching and encouraging the churches? (See Acts 16:3–5.)

Reflection

God often chooses the most unlikely candidates to accomplish great things for him—Moses, David, Ruth, Esther, a few young fishermen from Galilee, a zealous Pharisee, and yes, even a *mamzer*.

What does it mean to you to realize that even when you may not appear to "measure up," God can still use you in a special way to further his kingdom?

How do you think Timothy felt when Paul chose him, a *mamzer*, to be a disciple who would learn to walk as Jesus walked?

When you consider that Timothy's father was a Greek, and most likely not a believer, what effect do you think being considered Paul's "son" had on Timothy?

Why is it important for us to remember that God often uses unlikely disciples to do great things for his kingdom? To remember that God is always looking for Timothys who know Scripture, are filled with his Spirit, and will obey Jesus passionately as they learn to walk as Jesus walked?

Who is the outsider in your faith community who needs another disciple to recognize his or her passion for God and to offer to be an example of what it means to walk as Jesus walked?

why christians suffer: The weight of gethsemane

We are familiar with the cross. We wear it around our necks. We artistically celebrate it in wood, stone, and stained glass. We stand with the community of Jesus from ancient times in honoring the cross, and we profess a crucified Messiah in song and creed. We love that old rugged cross, the symbol of our relationship with God and the sign of our entrance into heaven.

But how closely does what the cross symbolizes for us resemble what it meant to Jesus and his disciples? Jesus must have shocked his disciples with the words, "If anyone would come [walk] after me, he must deny himself and take up his cross and follow me" (Matthew 16:24). They knew all too well what the cross and crucifixion meant in their world. The Romans had honed their skills in torture and brutality. After soldiers sadistically flogged the condemned person and paraded him or her through the streets where passersby mocked, pitied, or wept, the person was hung on a cross. Those who were best at crucifixion could ensure three days of excruciating pain for their victims before they would succumb to the relief of death.

If Jesus' invitation to his disciples was not frightening enough, he demonstrated by his own example what "take up his cross" meant. He spent hours in anguished prayer, pressed to the breaking point with the knowledge of what he would have to bear. Then, in complete obedience to the will of the Father, he willingly took up his cross and poured out his life as a sacrifice for us.

So where do we stand two thousand years later? We may desire to be his disciples, but do we really want to "take up our cross"? It seems we much prefer a theology that keeps crosses far away. The idea that we must do what Jesus did offends us. We're far more comfortable believing in a Jesus who went to the cross so we would not have to. *After all, we think, he was Messiah, the promised Savior. He had to suffer so we could receive eternal life.*

By the grace of God this is true. Our "cross" will never have the meaning of Jesus' cross. He "took up his cross" as a sacrifice for the sins of the world. Yet his call to discipleship demands that we imitate him and that means we also must take up our cross. This is an unpopular message in a culture that glorifies comfort and leisure and leaves no stone, or pill, unturned to avoid pain. Yet God calls us to be disciples—*talmidim* who passionately and obediently seek to imitate our Rabbi in every way.

If we desire to be disciples who make disciples, we *must* take up the cross. We must be willing to sacrifice and suffer in his name for what we believe. We must be willing to identify with those he came to love—the unlovable. We must be willing to be unpopular because our walk with Jesus will indict our cross-free culture.

Peter, one of Jesus' disciples, wrote, "Christ suffered for you, leaving you an example, that you should follow in his steps" (1 Peter 2:21). Peter chose to follow in the steps of Jesus. He died, tradition tells us, on a cross. Many of our ancient brothers and sisters in the faith followed in those same steps. They took the words of Jesus seriously and willingly took up the cross even when they knew that following in the steps of the Rabbi would lead to death. Let's see how their faithful example encourages us to follow Jesus' ancient command, "Take up *your* cross and follow me!"

opening Thoughts (4 minutes)

The Very Words of God

> *To this you were called, because Christ suffered for you, leaving you an example, that you should follow in his steps.*
>
> 1 Peter 2:21

Think About It

What do you think Jesus meant when he said that anyone who comes after him "must deny himself and take up his cross and follow me" (Mark 8:34)? How might your understanding of these words and their implication to your walk of faith differ from what Jesus' disciples understood them to mean?

DVD Notes (23 minutes)

Cappadocia

Images of Gethsemane

The call of a Rabbi who suffered

Echoes of those who followed the Rabbi

DVD Highlights (4 minutes)

1. A *gethsemane* is a powerful image in lands where olives are essential to everyday life. In what ways does Jesus' last visit to Gethsemane represent the suffering he willingly endured for you?

2. In what ways do you agree or disagree with the observation that taking up one's cross and following Jesus is not popular among Christians today—that we'd rather Jesus carry his cross so we don't have to?

   If this is our perspective, how does it affect our walk with Jesus?

3. What were your thoughts and feelings as you saw the early church carved out of the rock of Cappadocia and realized the great persecution of the believers who worshiped there? As you heard the testimonies of martyred believers who suffered because of their passionate obedience to God and devotion to Jesus?

   In what ways do their testimonies challenge or encourage you?

Data File
Olives, Oil, and Gethsemane

The word *gethsemane* is the English transliteration of a Greek word derived from two Hebrew (or Aramaic) words: *gat* or *gath* meaning "a place for pressing oil or wine," and *shemanim* meaning "oils." So, a *gethsemane* is an olive (or oil) press.

People in the Middle East harvest ripe, blackened olives in October and early November. During Jesus' time, olives designated for oil were placed in a crushing basin in which a large millstone rolled in a circle, crushing the olives—pits and all—into pulp. The pulp was then placed into shallow (about four inches tall and two feet in diameter) woven baskets (like rough burlap). The baskets of pulp were stacked on top of each other over (or in) a collecting pit. Usually made of solid rock, these pits were often located in the floor of a cave. Stone weights or a large stone pillar were then placed on top of the pulp, which gradually squeezed the oil into the pit or vat below.

Anyone who has seen streams of golden oil pouring from baskets in the many small oil presses still used in the Middle

East can understand why olive oil was a symbol of fertility and blessing in the ancient world. The oil's rich, pungent odor permeates the air for miles. The first pressing produces the best oil, which was an ingredient in many foods. Olive oil was also taken as medicine, used in skin care, and burned as lamp fuel.

Olive presses such as the very large press above, frequently were located in caves because the more moderate temperatures improved the efficiency of oil production. Apparently the press near the Mount of Olives where Jesus often went was so large that the surrounding area became known as "Gethsemane." The press would have been idle at the time Jesus was arrested because Passover is in the springtime.

small Group Bible Discovery and Group Discussion (18 minutes)

Understanding Gethsemane

The anguish Jesus bore in the olive grove known as Gethsemane on the night before his crucifixion provides a profound picture of God's love, Jesus' humanity, and the awful price to be paid for sin. Jesus suffered greatly as he anticipated the weight under which he would be pressed during the coming hours. He would be rejected by his friends, tried by religious leaders, tortured by Gentiles, brutally scourged, crucified, and—worst of all—rejected by God the Father as he suffered the agonies of hell for those he loved. It is impossible for us to fully understand the depth of Jesus' sorrow and pain during that time, but the images of a *gethsemane* provide a meaningful portrayal of his suffering. Let's take a closer look at the scene as it is recorded in Matthew 26:36–46, Mark 14:32–42, and Luke 22:39–46.

1. Who accompanied Jesus to Gethsemane and why did they go there? (See Mark 14:32–34.)

2. Consider Jesus' outlook that night and why he wanted his disciples to be with him. (See Matthew 26:36–38, 42–44; Mark 14:35–41.)

   a. Do you think it was unusual for Jesus to tell his disciples that he was "overwhelmed with sorrow to the point of death"? Why? What might they have thought when he said this?

b. How did Jesus' disciples respond to him during his time of need? What might they have felt and thought as, later in life, they looked back on the events of that evening in Gethsemane?

c. What indications do we see of the earnestness with which Jesus prayed that night? In what he asked God to do? In the language he used? In the number of times he returned to prayer? (See especially Matthew 26:42–44; Mark 14:35–36.)

Did You Know?

In Jewish tradition, a cup was shared after the meal called "the cup of Elijah." Based on Psalm 75:8 and Malachi 4, this cup represented the terrible judgment of God which would fall on sinners on the day of the Lord. This "cup of God's judgment" may be the background to Jesus' plea that the "cup" pass from him.

The Aramaic term *Abba* (Mark 14:36) is an affectionate expression for father—similar to what the word *Daddy* is in English. To this day, Jewish children refer to their fathers as *Abba*.

---

3. The descriptions of Jesus in prayer, his actions and demeanor, and his interaction with his disciples help portray his human nature and the staggering weight he carried the night before his crucifixion. Read Matthew 26:39–41, 53–54 and Luke 22:39–46, then discuss the following questions.

a. What temptation(s) might Jesus have faced during this time of suffering?

b. How intensely did Jesus feel the pressure?

c. How do we know from these accounts that Jesus completely submitted himself to the will of God the Father and poured himself out as an offering for the sins of the world? How did God respond to him?

4. In what ways was the mind-set of the disciples in Gethsemane so different from that of Jesus?

Were they being *talmidim* that night? Why or why not?

In what ways might the events of that night have affected their future walk with Jesus?

For Greater Understanding ...

In the language of biblical imagery, olives are a sign of God's blessing and anointing. Jesus' sweat at Gethsemane symbolizes the precious oil of God's anointing. The drops of blood were pressed out of Jesus by the weight of our sin—a burden he willingly bore because of his great love for each one of us. His blood, shed in his atoning death on the cross, anoints all who follow him, providing forgiveness, cleansing, and wholeness (see Ephesians 1:7–8; Colossians 1:19–20; Revelation 1:4–6).

faith Lesson (5 minutes)

1. In what ways do the images of a *gethsemane*—the crushing and pressing of the olives and the precious, golden oil that results—help you appreciate what Jesus endured for you?

2. How do the hours Jesus spent in prayer and the anguish and sorrow he felt in Gethsemane shape your understanding of God's love for you?

3. What does the example Jesus set in Gethsemane mean to you as you seek to be his disciple and walk as he walked? In what ways does his example better prepare you to face suffering?

closing (1 minute)

Thank God for his great love as Jesus demonstrated it in Gethsemane. Pray that you will be willing and faithful to walk as Jesus walked no matter what suffering you may be called to bear.

Memorize

To this you were called, because Christ suffered for you, leaving you an example, that you should follow in his steps.

1 Peter 2:21

walk as Jesus walked

In-Depth Personal Study Sessions

Day one/Take up your cross

The Very Words of God

Then Jesus said to his disciples, "If anyone would come after me, he must deny himself and take up his cross and follow me."

Matthew 16:24

Bible Discovery

Jesus' Followers Must Expect to Suffer

When Jesus said that anyone who would follow him must "take up his cross," he knew that doing so would lead to suffering and even death. But when he called his disciples from the towns of Galilee, they didn't suspect that following Jesus would lead them to walk by the way of the cross. They knew only that they had been called to follow their beloved Rabbi, and they eagerly accepted the opportunity.

As the disciples took on the "yoke" of Jesus (his interpretation and teaching of the Hebrew text that they knew and loved), they learned to follow in his footsteps. Day by day they fed their desire to be like him in every way, and when, after his death and resurrection they at last realized the path of suffering their Rabbi had chosen, they did not turn back. As *talmidim*, they faithfully followed his example and—willingly, joyfully, without reservation—took up their cross even when it led to suffering and death. What does this mean for Jesus' followers today? Does this high calling still apply to us? Consider what the text says.

1. To what extent did Jesus expect his disciples to follow him and be like him? (See Luke 6:40; John 12:26.)

2. Make a list of the things that people who want to be like Jesus more than anything else in the world will do. (See John 8:31; 13:12–17; 1 Peter 2:4–6; 1 John 2:4–6.)

3. What is the most amazing thing Jesus did for us? Why did he do it? (See John 3:14–17; 10:14–18; 15:13; 19:17–18.) If those who follow Jesus are to become like him in all things, do you think this means we must be willing to lay down our lives as well? Why or why not?

4. What does Scripture tell us about following Jesus in every way—even if it means suffering or death? How strongly did Jesus state this? (See Matthew 10:37–39; 16:24–25; Luke 14:26–27.) What do you think Jesus' disciples first thought when Jesus said they would need to take up their cross? How seriously did they take his words?

5. Obviously we don't accomplish the work of salvation if we die for our faith. Only the sacrificial death of Jesus could accomplish that. But what do we accomplish if we die because we walk as Jesus walked? (See John 15:10–13, 18–23.)

Reflection

Jesus warned his disciples that following him would lead to suffering. Reread John 15:18–21, and consider how his words would have prepared and strengthened them to take up their cross. What do these words mean to you?

What does taking up *your* cross require in your world?

In what way(s) might you be avoiding taking up your cross? What kinds of things (goals, secret thoughts, fears, and the like) hinder you from taking up your cross?

How badly do you really want to be like Jesus? What are the consequences if you try to follow him but are unwilling to take up your cross?

Ask God to open your mind and heart so you can hear and receive the ancient call to discipleship: "Take up your cross and follow." Ask him for the grace and passion to be like Jesus no matter what the cost.

Day Two/persecution — The Disciples' Gethsemane

The Very Words of God

Remember the words I spoke to you: "No servant is greater than his master." If they persecuted me, they will persecute you also. If they obeyed my teaching, they will obey yours also. They will treat you this way because of my name, for they do not know the One who sent me.

John 15:20–21

Bible Discovery

Three Sources of Persecution

Early Christian disciples of Jesus often were persecuted for their faith, although the persecution rarely affected the entire Roman Empire. Even so, many thousands of believers died. Others experienced deep suffering—physical, economic, emotional—because of their passionate commitment to Jesus and his teaching. Persecution came from within the Jewish community, from local Roman authorities, and from Imperial Rome.

1. Sometimes Jewish authorities persecuted early Christians. This usually occurred on a local level and consisted primarily of beatings, expulsion from synagogues, and shunning within the Jewish community. Occasionally these persecutions resulted in death. As you read about a few of these events, note what the concerns or issues were, how Jesus' followers suffered, how they used the opportunity to teach about Jesus, and what impact their example had on others.

   a. Acts 4:1–21; 5:12–42

b. Acts 6:8–15; 7:54–58 (If you are willing to take the time, read Stephen's entire defense, recorded in Acts 7:1–53.)

c. Acts 17:1–13

d. Acts 21:27–22:1, 22–25 (Again, if you are willing, read the entire account from Acts 21:27 to Acts 26:32 when Paul is sent to Rome to appeal to Caesar.)

2. What had Jesus told his disciples concerning persecution from local Jewish authorities? How would his words have prepared and strengthened his disciples? (See Matthew 10:17–20; 23:13, 34–36.)

3. Based on personal whims, local situations, or political convenience, local authorities in the Roman world at times persecuted Christians. These persecutions were more frequent but less widespread than the Imperial persecutions. In some cases, mobs killed untold numbers of early believers during riots regarding local issues. In North Africa, for example, a second-century riot in Smyrna resulted in the death of Polycarp, the bishop.

As you read about several local persecutions recorded in Scripture, note what was behind the persecution, what the officials were trying to accomplish, and the impact on the local community and the community of believers.

    a. Acts 12:1–19

    b. Acts 16:16–40

    c. Acts 19:23–41

4. How had Jesus encouraged and warned his disciples concerning the persecution they would face from various local authorities? (See Luke 12:4–12.)

Fact File

Roman authorities accused Jesus' followers of: rejecting the gods, cannibalism, incest, treason, anti-temple activities, causing economic loss (such as lost sales of idols), lack of patriotism, causing disasters by not supporting the gods, and undermining the social order.

5. Imperial Rome's persecution of Christians was far bloodier than other sources of persecution, but times of persecution from Rome rarely lasted for very long. Nevertheless, untold thousands of Jesus' followers suffered loss of property and rights, were sold into slavery, and were killed in extremely barbaric ways. Most of the information we have regarding these persecutions comes from the historical rather than the biblical record, but Acts 18:1–3 reveals one such persecution by the Emperor Claudius. How did God use this persecution to further his purposes? (See Acts 18:18–19, 24–28.)

    NOTE: The expulsion of Jews from Rome did not distinguish between Christian Jews and Jews who did not follow Jesus.

Data File
Roman Emperors Who Persecuted Christians

Claudius (AD 41–54). Expelled Christians from Rome.

Nero (AD 54–68). Persecution occurred mainly in Rome, and thousands of Jesus' disciples were killed. Church tradition records that Paul was beheaded and Peter was crucified in Rome during this time.

Domitian (AD 81–96). An extremely bloody and widespread campaign directed at Christians throughout the Empire. John was on Patmos during this persecution.

Trajan (AD 98–117). Empirewide persecution, which killed Ignatius, the bishop of Antioch.

Marcus Aurelius (AD 161–180). Executed Polycarp the bishop of Smyrna; killed entire communities of believers in Lyons and Vindobona (modern-day Vienna) as well as many other believers.

Septimius Severus (AD 193–211). Persecution extended to Roman province of North Africa.

Maximinus (AD 235–238). Little is known about this particular persecution.

Decius (AD 249–251). During this persecution, Cyprian the bishop of Carthage and Origen were tortured.

Valerian (AD 253–260). Little is known about this particular persecution.

Aurelian (AD 270–275). Little is known about this particular persecution.

Diocletian (AD 284–305). Began furiously persecuting Christians in 303; burned churches filled with Christians and also resorted to book burnings, torture, demolition of churches, and brutal executions; large number of believers were killed.

NOTE: Eusebius, who wrote *Church History*, was an eyewitness to Diocletian's persecutions of Christians and is an excellent source of information about persecution and martyrdom.

Reflection

As you consider the accounts of persecution highlighted above, what are your thoughts about Jesus' disciples and the early Christian believers? What were they willing to do when they were "pressed" by persecution?

What do you think enabled them to remain faithful to Jesus? How might their awareness of Jesus' own example and his warnings that they too would be persecuted have impacted them?

Does it surprise you that the message of Christ continued to be well received during intense times of persecution? Why or why not?

In what ways do you think persecution helps Christians become true disciples?

How does what Jesus suffered and what the early disciples suffered help you face the possibility of persecution and suffering in your life? Thank God for their faithful example and commitment to walk as Jesus walked.

Memorize

In fact, everyone who wants to live a godly life in Christ Jesus will be persecuted.

2 Timothy 3:12

Day Three/The Fruit of Suffering

The Very Words of God

... Though now for a little while you may have had to suffer grief in all kinds of trials. These have come so that your faith—of greater worth than gold, which perishes even though refined by fire—may be proved genuine and may result in praise, glory and honor when Jesus Christ is revealed.

1 Peter 1:6–7

Bible Discovery

Why Do We Suffer?

When we begin to look at how Jesus suffered and the suffering of those who faithfully followed him and shared his message with the world, we can't help but ask, "Why did they suffer so much?" People have struggled for millennia to understand why the righteous suffer, and, because God's thoughts are not our thoughts, we may never fully comprehend the purpose of suffering as God reveals it. We can know for certain that those who follow Jesus should expect suffering: Jesus told us it would come. And, in the heritage of suffering left to us by those who walked as Jesus walked, we see evidence of the fruit that suffering can produce.

1. Although it's painful to suffer for walking as Jesus walked, suffering can be instrumental in our spiritual development. Paul and the disciples of Jesus knew this, and they frequently shared this perspective with their disciples. They also taught their disciples to rejoice in suffering and encouraged them to focus their attention on the fruit it could produce. Read the following passages, taking note of the writers' perspectives on suffering, the promise of benefit in suffering, and the enduring hope of suffering.

    a. How did Paul view his suffering? (See Colossians 1:24–29.)

    b. In what eternal things can we hope when we suffer? What is some of the fruit of our suffering? (See 1 Peter 1:3–9.)

    c. What is the joy of suffering for Christ? How does God view our suffering for him? (See 1 Peter 4:12–16.)

    d. For what reasons can we be glad when we suffer for Jesus' sake? (See Matthew 5:10–12.)

    e. What is the fruit of suffering? What is the hope of suffering? (See Romans 5:1–5.)

    f. What do trials develop in the believer, and what should be our attitude toward them? (See James 1:1–4.)

2. How would you describe the attitude of the early Christian disciples toward their suffering? How does their attitude differ from yours? From that of other believers you know?

Reflection

The Scriptures teach us certain truths about suffering for Jesus' sake. Several of these have been summarized in the chart on page 145. Prayerfully think about each one and what it means to you and your daily walk with Jesus. Consider the challenges, the encouragement, and the steps you need to take in order to more closely follow your Rabbi. Pray about aspects of suffering for Jesus' sake that are confusing to you, that frighten you, or that seem too difficult. Passion for walking as Jesus walked comes not only from faithful obedience but from close communion with him regarding the desires of your heart.

Summary	What this means to me as I live my life
Those of us who desire to walk as Jesus walked will be persecuted.	
Jesus' call to follow him demands a willingness to suffer because he asks us to "take up" our "cross."	
Suffering for Christ gives us the privilege of joining him in his suffering.	
Persecution for Christ purifies us to be more holy for God and his purposes.	
Suffering for Christ enables us to experience the grace he gives us moment by moment.	
Suffering for Christ joins us with remarkable disciples of Jesus from the past who faithfully followed him no matter what the price.	

Does knowing these truths make suffering for Jesus less painful? Why or why not?

Does knowing these truths help us see purpose in our suffering? Why or why not?

What are some examples of times when we experience pain in order to accomplish a greater good (for instance, giving birth or sacrificing to help a needy family)? In what ways do these experiences encourage you to "welcome" the opportunity to suffer for Jesus?

For Greater Understanding ...
Olives in the Bible

Olive trees and olive oil played a significant role throughout the ancient Middle East, including during the time of Jesus and the early Christian disciples. So it is not surprising that images of olive trees and oil appear in Scripture as symbols of spiritual truth. Some of these images relate to God's desire for the lives of his people to bear fruit.

Consider the unusual characteristics of the olive tree, for example. Olive trees rarely reach twenty feet high, but they can bear fruit for more than a hundred years. When an olive tree gets very old and stops bearing, the branches are cut off. Soon new shoots grow out of the stump, which can survive for centuries, and the tree begins producing olives again.

Isaiah used this characteristic of olive trees to provide an image for his prophecy: "A shoot will come up from the stump of Jesse; from his roots a Branch will bear fruit" (Isaiah 11:1). Jesus was the shoot, the "Branch" from the stump of Jesse (David's father).

In Romans 11:11–24, Paul used this characteristic of the olive tree to illustrate God's plan of salvation. He described Christians as either being natural branches (those of Jewish background) or branches (meaning Gentiles) that have been grafted onto the stump that is Jesus. Like branches on an olive tree, believers who are "attached" to Jesus, who draw their life from him, will bear fruit.

Jesus used images of the olive tree in his teaching as well. In Matthew 7:15–20 he warned against false teachers who do not produce good fruit and said they would be cut down. He also said that people can be recognized for who they are by the fruit they produce.

Olive oil is one of the great blessings of the olive tree. In Scripture, olive oil represents God's Spirit and the process of anointing. Acts 10:38 described Jesus as God's anointed one who was filled with the Holy Spirit and "went around doing good and healing all who were under the power of the devil, because God was with him." And in 1 John 2:20, those who follow Jesus are also described as being anointed by the Holy One.

What a privilege it is to be anointed with God's Spirit and to do good and bear fruit as we follow in the footsteps of the Rabbi!

Day four/cappadocia:
Hope in the midst of suffering

The Very Words of God

They were stoned; they were sawed in two; they were put to death by the sword. They went about in sheepskins and goatskins, destitute, persecuted and mistreated — the world was not worthy of them. They wandered in deserts and mountains, and in caves and holes in the ground.

Hebrews 11:37–38

Did You Know?

Cappadocia was known in ancient times as a place to hide. Its unique geography—a moderately high plain surrounded by mountains on three sides—made access difficult from all directions except the west. Once in the region, however, travelers could easily traverse the rolling, treeless plain. The land was very fertile and suitable for vineyards and grain farming, which supported a locally based agricultural economy rather than a trade-based economy. This and the lack of cities further isolated the region from the rest of the world. The land also has a number of rocky canyons where people can live in hiding. The sparse population, isolation, local landscape, and fertility of the volcanic soil made it possible for refugees who reached Cappadocia to live anonymously.

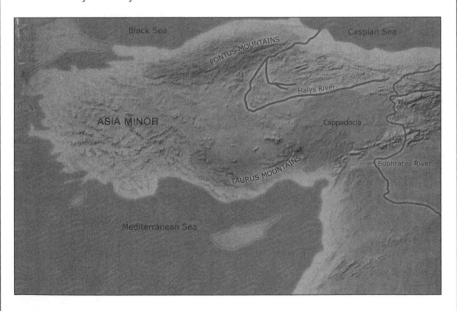

Bible Discovery

The Christian Movement in Cappadocia

We don't know exactly how the message of Jesus arrived in Cappadocia, but there is evidence that a community of Jesus' disciples lived there early in the first century. Peter apparently spent time in the region because he addressed his first epistle to believers in Cappadocia as well as in regions to the west. His letters include references to persecution, so it may be that Roman persecution forced many believers into hiding there. Even the language of his letters—*scattered, suffering, aliens,* and *strangers*—fits Cappadocia well. After all, for thousands of years these words accurately described people who lived in Cappadocia.

1. When might the Christian movement in Cappadocia have started? What does Acts 2:5–11 reveal about the Jewish communities in Cappadocia?

2. Read the 1 Peter Scripture passages below and on page 50, keeping in mind that Peter wrote these words to encourage believers who had faced, were facing, or could soon face persecution and suffering. Look for every source of hope and consider what it would mean to people who were personally acquainted with persecution.

Scripture Passage	Message of Hope	Meaning for Those Who Suffer
1 Peter 1:1–7		
1 Peter 2:11–12, 20–23		

1 Peter 3:14 – 17		
1 Peter 5:8 – 11		

Profile of a Village: Nyssa

This DVD session was filmed in Cappadocia near the contemporary village of Zelve, which was known as Nyssa during ancient times. Roman persecution forced many of Jesus' followers to flee to remote canyons or underground complexes where they could live in rooms carved out of the thick layer of *tufa* that blankets Cappadocia. Tufa is a soft rock of volcanic ash that is easy to carve and hardens when it is exposed to air. In some places this layer is hundreds of feet thick, so it is possible to carve out entire communities within the tufa layer. Consider what it was like to live in the tufa.

- Some communities were carved into the walls of canyons where the tufa had been eroded by wind and water. Other communities on the plains were carved deep into the ground (as deep as 280 feet!).
- Cavelike dwellings carved into the tufa enabled inhabitants to moderate their exposure to the extreme summer heat and bitter winter cold for which Cappadocia is known.
- The dwellings carved into the canyons often had two or more levels connected by tunnels and shafts.
- Larger rooms and community areas (such as places of worship) had arched ceilings so the ceilings wouldn't collapse.

- When Roman persecution stopped, entire communities of Jesus' followers continued to live in the caves of Cappadocia to avoid the corrupting influences of the Hellenistic Roman culture.

The canyon near Nyssa (shown in bottom photo) is one place we know Christians inhabited. In fact, by the fourth century, after persecution by the Romans stopped, this valley had become a center of the Christian monastic movement. More than 3,500 ancient churches have been discovered here.

Reflection

Suffering, joy, and hope may seem incompatible to us—but not for the disciple who walks as Jesus walked! Read 1 Peter 4:1–2, 12–16 and prayerfully consider Peter's message of hope in the midst of suffering.

Who has suffered physically before us? (verse 1)

What change in life perspective happens when we suffer for Jesus? (verse 2)

What is Peter's perspective on the presence of suffering in the life of a believer? (verse 12) In what ways does his perspective differ from yours?

How might your experience of suffering be different if you viewed it as normal rather than an unacceptable intrusion into your life?

What is the great privilege of suffering for Christ? (verse 13)

How committed a disciple must you be to actually rejoice in the privilege of sharing in Christ's suffering? How do you think the early disciples viewed this opportunity and why? How do you view this opportunity, and what does your perspective say about your desire to walk as Jesus walked?

What gives us hope in the midst of suffering? (verses 13–16)

Memorize

Rejoice that you participate in the sufferings of Christ, so that you may be overjoyed when his glory is revealed.

1 Peter 4:13

Day five/Listen to the Echoes

The Very Words of God

If you suffer as a Christian, do not be ashamed, but praise God that you bear that name.

1 Peter 4:16

Bible Discovery

What Echoes Will You Leave Behind?

This session has followed the ancient footsteps of our Christian brothers and sisters, some of whom lived in a remote valley of cave dwellings in Cappadocia. There, in a church carved by hand out of solid rock, we heard the echoes of ordinary disciples who took Jesus seriously. They took up their cross. Willingly, joyfully, they followed the Rabbi even when the path led to death. There are no plaques, monuments, or modern signs that honor their faithfulness, but there is no mistaking the echoes of their message! We can still hear those echoes loud and clear in Jesus' ancient command: "Take up *your* cross and follow me!"

1. Jesus' disciples took seriously their commitment to take up their cross and follow him. They lived it, they taught it, and they died because of it. In the spaces below, notice what two New Testament writers taught their disciples about suffering for Jesus' sake.

Writer and Bible Passage	Echoes of Their Walk with Jesus
Paul 2 Tim. 3:10–12	
Peter 1 Peter 4:12–16, 19	
Paul Phil. 3:8–12	

2. What did these passages mean to early believers, for whom ongoing persecution and suffering was a real possibility? How would these messages have encouraged them to endure persecution?

3. Why do you think so many early believers followed Jesus knowing that they would pay a high price for walking as he walked?

4. What do these verses mean to us today? To what extent are we willing to "share" with Jesus in his suffering, as so many of the early believers did?

The Wisdom of the Rabbis

A Jewish rabbi once said, "A great martyr is not someone with the courage to die for what he believes, but someone with the courage to live passionately for God every day of his life."

I love that thought. If we live for God every moment, we can be sure that he will give us the grace to do so when suffering comes. If we do not live for him, I am not sure we can count on such grace.

Ray Vander Laan

Reflection

Just as we have heard echoes of the steps of faithful believers from the first century, believers of the future will hear the echoes of our walk of faith today.

What will they hear? Will the echoes of our footsteps as we follow the Rabbi strengthen and encourage them to walk as Jesus walked no matter what the cost? Or will they hear our steps falter and fade into the din of a culture that does not know the Rabbi?

The choice is ours. What price are you willing to pay to take up your cross and follow Jesus?

Memorize

Blessed are those who are persecuted because of righteousness, for theirs is the kingdom of heaven.

Matthew 5:10

Don't forget us

I don't think Jesus is going to return soon," stated a high school girl during a class I (Ray) teach in a Christian school.

"Why not?" I asked.

"Because Jesus said ..." (and here she paused, knowing the importance of quoting the Bible accurately), "he said, 'Then you will be handed over to be persecuted and put to death, and you will be hated by all nations because of me ... and then the end will come' [Matthew 24:9, 14b]. Jesus can't return yet because we are not being persecuted. He said so."

Silence hung heavy in the classroom. Students and I looked over at two young women from Sudan, West Africa. Tears streamed down one's face; the other stared out of the window, nearly in tears. We knew their story. Muslim raiders from northern Sudan had brutally plundered followers of Jesus in the south. These teenagers had seen their families and friends slaughtered and their churches burned. Like many other children, they walked hundreds of miles to the relative safety of a refugee camp in another country. Eventually, through support of Christians in the West, they came to the United States and started new lives. Some do not even know if any other family members are alive.

"I'm sorry," the girl who had spoken said tearfully, looking at her two classmates. "I guess we *are* suffering." She had not meant to overlook the suffering of these Christians. But, like many of us, because she was not being persecuted, it was easy to forget the suffering of Christians who are. As a class, we gathered around our Sudanese friends, put our hands on them, and prayed, deeply moved by their pain.

"What do you wish from us, your Christian brothers and sisters from the West?" I asked.

One Sudanese girl softly replied, "Don't forget us."

Her words still echo in my mind. Of course God said that when one member of Jesus' body in the world suffers, we all suffer. How easy it is, though, to pay attention only to what happens in our little region of the world. We do not easily feel the pain of brothers and sisters who live outside our communities of faith, who speak other languages and live in other cultures and in other times. Our sense of the body of Christ often is quite shallow.

This session is part of the commitment I made not to forget them. It not only explores the suffering of Jesus' body many years ago, it is also a testimony to the courage and passion for Jesus that I have experienced through several young disciples of Jesus from the Sudan. Together we are the body of Christ, past and present. And this body is suffering *today*. May God's grace strengthen us.

opening Thoughts (4 minutes)

The Very Words of God

We know that we have come to know him if we obey his commands. . . .
Whoever claims to live in him must walk as Jesus did.

1 John 2:3, 6

Think About It

As you go about your daily life, how often do you think about your fellow believers who have suffered (and are suffering) because they chose to walk with Jesus? Do you ever think that God wants their suffering to have a meaningful impact on your life? Why or why not?

DVD Notes (23 minutes)

Following the Rabbi in Derinkuyu

God's plan for those who follow and suffer

Is the body of Christ suffering?

Rebecca's story

Don't forget

DVD Highlights (4 minutes)

1. As you saw images of the underground city beneath the village of Derinkuyu, what do you think it would have been like to live there with your family for a week? For a month? For more than a year? Honestly talk about whether that kind of life is a sacrifice you (and your loved ones) would gladly make in your efforts to walk with Jesus.

One of hundreds of steep, narrow tunnels in Derinkuyu

2. Ray Vander Laan spoke about how when one part of our body is injured, even if it is just our little finger, our whole body feels and responds to the pain. In what ways did his illustration increase your awareness of what it means to suffer as the body of Christ?

3. What did you feel when Rebecca shared her story?

What did she help you realize about suffering in the body of Christ?

What would you like to do in response to the pain and suffering she has endured for the cause of Christ?

small Group Bible Discovery and Group Discussion (18 minutes)

Persecution: Time to Stand or Time to Run?

What is required for believers to walk as Jesus walked when they face persecution? According to tradition, believers in ancient Ephesus refused to leave when the Romans began enforcing emperor worship, and many of them were killed because of their commitment to Christ. In other places, believers sacrificed everything they owned and fled to remote places such as the cave cities of Cappadocia. Even the disciples of Jesus fled persecution in some instances and boldly confronted it in others. Does one choice demonstrate a greater commitment to Jesus than the other? Let's look to the Scriptures to see how Jesus' disciples responded when they were persecuted.

1. Peter and John were preaching in Jerusalem where thousands of people believed their message. The Sadducees (the powerful religious leaders who were aligned with the Roman authorities) objected to their preaching the resurrection of the dead, so they had Peter and John arrested. (See Acts 4:1–3, 18–21, 29–31.)

    a. What impact did being jailed for teaching the message of Jesus have on Peter and John? Why did they respond as they did?

    b. What did Peter, John, and other believers pray for after their release? How does their response show us that it was very important to them to continue walking as Jesus walked? In what way did the body of Christ share in their sufferings?

2. When Peter and the other apostles were arrested in Jerusalem, what did God tell them to do, and how did they respond? How important did they think it was to continue walking as Jesus walked? (See Acts 5:17–21, 28–29.)

3. Consider how Saul (Paul) and the followers of Jesus responded when his life was threatened in Damascus. (See Acts 9:23–30.)

   a. Once Saul was safe, what did he immediately begin doing?

   b. After his escape, was Saul any less committed to continue walking as Jesus walked? How do we know this?

   c. How did the body of Christ in Jerusalem respond to the threats against Saul? Do you think their actions demonstrated a commitment to obey God and walk as Jesus walked? Why or why not?

4. Read Acts 14:1–7, which records the persecution Paul and Barnabas faced in Iconium during their teaching tour in Galatia.

   a. What was their initial response to persecution? (verses 2–3)

   b. How did they respond when the persecution intensified? (verses 5–7)

c. Do you think they made a mistake in their initial response? Why or why not?

d. Did their commitment to preach the message of Jesus diminish in any way while they were in Iconium and after they left? What do you think motivated them to stay and face persecution at some times and to flee at other times?

Profile of an Underground City

The underground city of Derinkuyu in Cappadocia covers more than a square kilometer. It is believed to be the largest of twenty-five such communities in the region. The complex comprises twenty levels of chambers that are as deep as 280 feet below the surface! The name of this particular underground city, Derinkuyu, means "deep well," which is appropriate because a deep, working well provided some of its water supply. The well also served as an air shaft to help circulate air in the massive complex where as many as ten thousand people may have lived. A labyrinth of narrow passages and vertical shafts connected the hundreds of chambers in this complex. Other tunnels, as yet unopened, are believed to connect this complex to similar underground communities more than five miles away!

Derinkuyu started simply. Residents of the town on the surface would carve out a room under their homes to provide safe hiding places should an enemy appear. These rooms had hidden entrances, traps, and stone doors that made them difficult for an enemy to find or to move through. As needed, residents hollowed out new rooms and passageways. During thousands of years and numerous periods of persecution, these hiding places were enlarged and joined to form the large underground complexes we see today.

As persecution intensified and people lived in Derinkuyu for longer periods of time, the complex became much more sophisticated. It is, in many ways, an engineering marvel.

- Surface water from disguised holes was directed into cisterns at varying levels in the complex.
- Vertical shafts with handholds and footholds provided ventilation and enabled residents to communicate and move quickly between levels.
- Large millstones (three to six feet in diameter and twelve to sixteen inches thick) weighing as much as 1,200 pounds served as doors to block narrow tunnels and prevent enemies from progressing into the complex. These rolling doors were designed to be very difficult to roll back from the outside and often had small spaces where hot oil or spears could be used against an enemy trying to chisel through the stone door.

Specific chambers in the complex were designed for eating, sleeping, and other uses. Kitchen chambers were located on the upper levels and often had vents to the surface that were disguised as wells. Many ancient ovens are still intact as are some pottery jars with remnants of barley, wheat, vegetables, olive oil, and wine. Sometimes animals were kept in upper-level stables where pits were carved to store fodder and holes were carved into corners of the rock so the animals could be tied up.

Deep in the complex (240 feet) is the small church where Rebecca shared her story. The arched shape of the ceiling and cross shape of the space enabled the room to be larger without risking collapse of the structure. The entire space is about eighty feet long and fifteen feet wide, with the "T" part of the cross being about thirty-five feet wide. During times of persecution by the Romans and later Muslims and Persians, Christians came here to escape and worship God.

faith lesson (5 minutes)

1. On the day Stephen died for teaching the message of Jesus, per-
    secution of the early church began in earnest. Read Acts 8:1 – 4
    and consider the different ways followers of Jesus responded and
    what they suffered during this crisis. What would continuing to
    walk with Jesus have required of you if you had been in Jerusa-
    lem at that time?

2. As the early church grew and times of persecution continued,
    our brothers and sisters in Jesus sometimes left their homes and
    hid deep underground with their families rather than compro-
    mise their faith. Imagine their choice: to worship the Roman
    emperor and live in the sunshine, or remain disciples of Jesus
    and suffer underground. What would you have done? What sac-
    rifices are worth making to walk as Jesus walked?

3. If you are a believer, how has what you learned today influenced
    your understanding of and commitment to being a courageous
    disciple regardless of the suffering you may face?

closing (1 minute)

Being a disciple and making disciples always carries the possibility of persecution and suffering. Whether we make our stand where we are and suffer or whether we flee and suffer, our call to be disciples who walk as Jesus walked and our assignment to make disciples does not change. Let's end this study in the Jewish way by reciting these words of Scripture together:

Memorize

> *Then Jesus came to them and said, "All authority in heaven and on earth has been given to me. Therefore go and make disciples of all nations, baptizing them in the name of the Father and of the Son and of the Holy Spirit, and teaching them to obey everything I have commanded you. And surely I am with you always, to the very end of the age."*
>
> Matthew 28:18–20

walk as jesus walked

In-Depth Personal Study Sessions

Day one/we are one body:
The body of christ

The Very Words of God

Just as each of us has one body with many members, and these mem-bers do not all have the same function, so in Christ we who are many form one body, and each member belongs to all the others.

Romans 12:4 – 5

Bible Discovery

Understanding the Unity of the Body

We talk about the church being the body of Christ, but our view of what that means is often very limited. We may consider ourselves to be brothers or sisters in Christ's body with the believers we know in our local church, in our neighborhoods, or at work, but our vision rarely goes beyond that. It is quite a stretch for us to see our connection in the body of Christ with Christians who live on the other side of the globe or who lived hundreds or thousands of years ago. And yet, in Christ, we are members with them of the same body. So let's consider what the early disciples understood the body of Christ to mean and see if we can broaden our awareness of what it means in light of our walk with Jesus.

1. As the Passover lamb and head of the church, Jesus left an indel-ible image to remind us of what he has done for us.

   a. What is this image? (See 1 Corinthians 11:23 – 26.)

b. How did Paul use this image to illustrate what it means to be part of Christ's body? (See 1 Corinthians 10:16–17.)

c. In light of Paul's understanding, what does taking Communion represent?

d. Is the significance of Communion limited to the early church, or does it have the same meaning for everyone throughout history who chooses to walk as Jesus walked? How does this realization alter your view of the body of Christ?

2. The teaching that those who follow Jesus become members of one body—his body—occurs throughout the letters to the early churches. Read Romans 12:4–5; 1 Corinthians 12:12–13, 21–27; Ephesians 1:22–23; and Colossians 1:18 and and note the following:

a. Who is the head of the body?

b. Who are the members of the body?

c. What is the relationship between the members of the body?

3. Paul passionately argued for unity among the body of Christ—all the followers of Jesus—and for the value of all members and their respective gifts. The following passages provide insight into why he considered the body of Christ to be so important.

    a. Who has made the body exactly what it is? (See 1 Corinthians 12:18–20; Ephesians 4:11.)

    b. What are the purposes of the body? (See Ephesians 4:11–13.)

    c. How does the body fulfill these purposes? (See Ephesians 4:15–16.)

Reflection

Read 1 Corinthians 12:12–13 and take a few moments to consider the implications of being part of the body of Christ as God has designed it.

> In what ways does your faith community function like the body of Christ described in 1 Corinthians 12? In what ways does it fail to function as it should? What do you think your God-given role is, as part of that body, to participate in building it up and preparing it for works of service?

Now think beyond your immediate faith community. Who are the other members of the body? Is every believer who has ever lived a member of Jesus' body? What, then, is your relationship to past and future believers? What do you think your God-given role is in building up the whole body of Christ and preparing it for works of service?

What happens to the part of the body with which you live in close proximity when strife, indifference, and dissension exist within its members? What happens to the whole body of Christ throughout history when strife, indifference, and dissension exist within its members?

Memorize

The body is a unit, though it is made up of many parts; and though all its parts are many, they form one body. So it is with Christ. For we were all baptized by one Spirit into one body — whether Jews or Greeks, slave or free — and we were all given the one Spirit to drink.

1 Corinthians 12:12 – 13

DAY TWO/we share in the suffering of christ's body

The Very Words of God

The body is a unit, though it is made up of many parts; and though all its parts are many, they form one body. So it is with Christ ... so that there should be no division in the body, but that its parts should have equal concern for each other. If one part suffers, every part suffers with it; if one part is honored, every part rejoices with it.

1 Corinthians 12:12, 25–26

Bible Discovery

The Body of Jesus Still Suffers Today

Jesus experienced great physical suffering in order to redeem sinful humanity. In one sense, his suffering ended with his resurrection and ascension back to his Father in heaven. In another sense, his body remains on earth and continues to suffer as the community of believers that make up his church. So the unity of the body of Jesus is essential not only to our understanding of how to walk as Jesus walked but to our understanding of suffering within the body of Jesus, the church. Consider how the early disciples viewed the sufferings of the body of Christ.

1. What were the sufferings of Jesus, and what did his suffering accomplish for all of humanity? (See Luke 9:22; Colossians 1:21–22; 1 John 2:1–2.)

2. Why was Jesus willing to suffer for the sins of every person? (See John 3:16–17; 10:14–16; Philippians 2:5–8; 1 Timothy 1:15–16.)

3. How do we know that those who follow Jesus will suffer? (See Matthew 16:24–25; John 13:15–16; 15:20.)

4. Why should those who walk with Jesus be willing to suffer? (See Philippians 2:1–5; 1 Peter 2:21.)

5. What is the relationship between one member of the body of Jesus who is suffering and the rest of the body? And how does God want the members of the body to respond to the members who are suffering? (See 1 Corinthians 12:25–26.)

To Keep in Mind

Jesus suffered persecution in order to redeem the world. The persecution that Jesus' earthly body—all believers, the church—suffers comes as a result of passionately following him. Because Jesus suffered, suffering is a part of walking as Jesus walked and becoming like him.

6. The suffering of the body of Jesus—the church—today does not accomplish salvation as the suffering of Jesus' physical body did. So what is the purpose of suffering in the body of Christ? What does the ongoing suffering of the body of Jesus accomplish?

Scripture	Purpose and Results of Suffering in the Body of Jesus
2 Thess. 1:3–5	
2 Tim. 1:8–12	
1 Peter 1:6–9	
1 Peter 4:12–14	

Reflection

Paul wrote about his suffering on behalf of the body of Christ in Colossians 1:24–29. Read this passage several times to grasp what he is saying about his suffering.

Why did Paul suffer for the body of Christ, and what was his attitude toward it? What surprises you about his attitude, and in what ways does it differ from yours?

Paul seemed eager to suffer for Christ in order to benefit the body—as he wrote, to "present everyone perfect in Christ." In what ways have you been the beneficiary of Paul's suffering? Do you want to have that same passionate concern for other believers? Why or why not?

If we are truly the body of Christ, and one person in the body suffers for his or her faith—whether it be in China or Africa, whether it be last week or tomorrow—who else is suffering?

How intensely do we really feel the pain of our brothers and sisters who, even today, are sacrificing their lives for their faith in Jesus? What keeps us from being aware of and responding to their pain?

When it is your turn to be a suffering member of the body, how might you feel if Christians in other places who are not suffering rarely think of you, don't pray for you, and don't advocate for you in whatever way they could?

Memorize

To this you were called, because Christ suffered for you, leaving you an example, that you should follow in his steps.

1 Peter 2:21

Day Three/Our Spiritual Inheritance

The Very Words of God

In fact, everyone who wants to live a godly life in Christ Jesus will be persecuted.

2 Timothy 3:12

Bible Discovery

A Heritage and Hope of Faith

Many Christians today use the word *faith* to describe an intellectual understanding of biblical truth, but intellect alone cannot make a person a true disciple. The Scriptures link faith to *action*—applying one's beliefs in everyday life. That is why being a disciple involves knowing God's Word *and* obeying it. Hebrews 11 outlines the heritage of faith passed down to us by the great men and women who put their belief into action daily and served God faithfully. They walked with God during good times as well as during times of great suffering. So take a closer look at this passage of Scripture to see the remarkable example of faith they have left for us to follow.

1. Read Hebrews 11:1–31.

   a. How is faith described in this chapter, and how does acting according to faith fit with this definition?

   b. How often is faith linked to action in this chapter? In what ways did these people demonstrate their faith? List them on the following page. What kinds of things did their faith accomplish? List them on the following page. Continue your lists on a separate page if needed. What amazes you about these two lists?

The Person of Faith	The Act of Faith	The Accomplishment of Faith

c. What did God often do in response to these actions of faith? How exciting for you is the realization that God commends his followers for their faith? In what ways is that a motivation to continue walking in faith?

d. What else motivated these people to live by faith? What reward did they look forward to? Did they receive what was promised while they were living?

2. Several times in Hebrews 11, the text mentions God rewarding his followers. How much does the hope of reward promised to Jesus' disciples influence your daily life and your willingness to speak boldly for Jesus?

3. The legacy of faith continues in Hebrews 11:32–38 although these faithful followers, for the most part, remain unnamed. If you read these carefully, you will probably be able to match names with many of these acts of the faithful.

a. In what ways did these people suffer for their faith?

b. What did some of them accomplish by faith?

c. How did the world treat them because of their faith? Might some of these faithful followers have been from Cappadocia?

**One of Cappadocia's narrow valleys where persecuted believers
carved out holes in the rock walls for shelter**

4. Hebrews 11:39–40 gives us insight into why these people suf-
    fered and endured in their faith. Study this passage to see how
    we, as followers of Jesus today, are a part of that picture.

    a. What did these faithful people receive?

    b. What didn't they receive, and why?

    c. Since the phrase, "would they be made perfect" means to "be
        complete," what is the connection between what we do for
        God today and the work these ancient believers started?

d. What impact does it have on you to realize that these ancient people of faith were willing to endure great suffering in order to pass on their faith to us?

e. How do their examples encourage you to live with a greater awareness of the members of the body of Jesus who are not yet born?

Reflection

Read Hebrews 12.1–3 in light of what you have learned from Hebrews 11. In what ways has this study strengthened your commitment to run your race of faith with diligence?

Now imagine that two Cappadocian martyrs come to you. They are excited because they know that you have received what they were willing to die in order to preserve—the Christian faith and what it means to be a disciple of Jesus. What would you say to them? What could you point to as an example of what you have done with your spiritual "inheritance"? Would you feel proud? Humble? Guilty? Embarrassed? Why?

What are you doing with the faith that persecuted believers from Cappadocia and many other places have passed on to you?

What kind of spiritual legacy—things of eternal value—will you pass on to those who will come after you? What will future generations hear in the echoes you leave behind?

Day Four/Trials and Persecution: Tests of a Disciple's Heart

The Very Words of God

Blessed is the man who perseveres under trial, because when he has stood the test, he will receive the crown of life that God has promised to those who love him.

James 1:12

Bible Discovery

A Disciple Will Be Tested

There are no easy answers to the question, "Why do Christians suffer?" Sometimes God gives us an answer; more often, we do not know. We do, however, know that those who follow Jesus suffer because Jesus did, because he asked us to, and because he predicted we would. We suffer because of the believers who suffered in order to give us the faith, and we suffer to pass on that faith to those who come after us. And we suffer because of our hope for the heavenly crown that awaits us.

Although we may never fully understand the whys of our suffering, we can be confident that our pain is not in vain. God promises that our suffering—the unexplained path of his people—has purpose and meaning. One of those purposes is to test the hearts of those who desire to walk as Jesus walked.

1. If we respond to the call of Jesus, the Rabbi who suffered so much for us, and accept his invitation to be his disciples, what should we expect to happen in our lives? Why? (See Luke 6:40; John 15:18–21; 1 John 2:6.)

   Are any of Jesus' disciples exempt from persecution and suffering? Why or why not?

2. What is the purpose for some of the suffering a disciple will face? (See Matthew 10:17–19.)

3. Testing the hearts of his people is nothing new to God. He has been doing it since the beginning of his relationship with the human race. Read the following passages and notice what each test was and what God wanted to accomplish through it.

Scripture Text	Nature of the Test	God's Purpose for the Test
Ex. 16:4–8, 16–20		
Ex. 20:18–21		

Deut. 8:1–6		
Judg. 2:20–23		
Zech. 13:9		

What do these tests show you about how important obedience is to God? About how much God loves his people? About God's commitment to those who follow him?

4. God's testing of the hearts of his people did not end with the coming of Jesus. If anything, the testing and the value of what it accomplished in the body of Christ intensified. Read the following passages and notice the severity of what was suffered and the results.

Scripture Text	The Intensity of the Suffering	What the Testing Accomplished
2 Cor. 1:8–11		
Heb. 5:7–10		
1 Peter 1:6–9		

5. According to 1 Corinthians 3:10–15, why does God allow intense testing of his people? What are the benefits and results of testing?

6. What reward is promised to disciples who faithfully endure testing? (See James 1:12.)

Reflection

God repeatedly calls David a man after his own heart. Read Psalm 26:1–8 and Psalm 139:23–24 and notice the attitude of David's heart toward being tested by God.

What did David pray for, and why?

Have you ever been bold enough to invite God to test you? Why or why not?

Is being tested something a disciple of Jesus should seek? Why or why not?

If you are a disciple whose greatest desire is to love the Lord your God with all your heart, soul, and strength, what adjustments do you need to make in your attitude and your response toward God when you are tested?

How much of a personal price are you willing to pay to receive the benefit(s) and reward that can come from being tested?

Memorize

Love the LORD *your God with all your heart and with all your soul and with all your strength.*

Deuteronomy 6:5

For Greater Understanding …

It's amazing to realize that God desires to use in significant ways every person who is willing to follow him faithfully. If you haven't already explored *Faith Lessons 6: In the Dust of the Rabbi*, please consider doing so because it complements these sessions well. It emphasizes the key practices of discipleship that will help you become an effective disciple of Jesus who, in turn, makes disciples as Jesus commanded. May you discover the joy of walking with the Messiah and learning to walk as he walked by:

Living in community

Remember the amazing presence of the communities
of faithful believers who lived for Jesus
in the pagan world of Asia Minor.
Acts 2:42–47
1 Peter 2:4–5

Following the Rabbi (Jesus) with great passion

Don't lose sight of the passion of Elijah.
Let his example inspire you to give everything you've got
to your walk with Jesus.
1 Kings 19:14
Matthew 16:13–14
Hebrews 12:1–3

Becoming a person of the text — knowing the Bible

Remember the faithful Jews of Galilee who expended great
effort to know the text. They loved the text, knew the text,
debated the text, taught the text, and lived the text.
Psalm 119:9–16
Luke 11:28

Becoming the body of Jesus

Pray for a keen awareness of what it means to participate
in the sufferings of Jesus and for a deepening sense of
community with believers of other times and cultures.
Matthew 16:24–25
Romans 12:4–5
Philippians 2:1–8

Imitating the Rabbi (Jesus) in your walk with God

A true disciple observes and imitates the Rabbi in everything
—even if it means walking on water like the Rabbi!—
in order to become as much like the Rabbi as possible.
John 15:9–17
1 John 2:3–6

Going and making disciples

Jesus is our example. Make disciples who follow him
and set the example for tomorrow's disciples.
Matthew 28:18–20
1 Corinthians 11:1–2

Refusing to forget believers who suffer for Jesus

Ask God to make you more sensitive to and appreciative of
the sufferings that other believers—such as Rebecca
and the unnamed Cappadocian martyrs—endure on your behalf.
1 Corinthians 12:12–14, 25–27
Philippians 4:10–14

Day Five/Don't Forget Us

The Very Words of God

*There should be no division in the body, but that its parts should have
equal concern for each other. If one part suffers, every part suffers
with it.*

1 Corinthians 12:25–26

Bible Discovery

Don't Forget

At the close of his letter of instruction to the body of Christ at
Colosse, Paul wrote, "Remember my chains. Grace be with you" (Colossians 4:18). Even though Paul had never met the believers in Colosse, he
longed for their support and care. His plea is the plea of all suffering and
persecuted members of the body of Christ. They long for the prayers,
encouragement, and support of other believers.

It has been estimated that more people were killed for Jesus' sake
during the twentieth century than during the nineteen centuries preceding it. Rebecca represents the tens of thousands of nameless, faceless followers of Jesus whose lives are at risk every day because they
walk with Jesus. Sadly, believers in the West have often overlooked the
magnitude of their suffering. But we must not forget! "If one part [of the
body] suffers, every part suffers with it" (1 Corinthians 12:26).

It isn't easy for those who are spared suffering and persecution to remember the persecuted, especially when the miles in between are many and our cultures are vastly different. But if we are suffering, we must know that the body of Christ everywhere suffers with us. And if we are spared persecution, we must remember the persecuted. We must enter their experience with prayer, encouragement, and whatever support we can offer. We have much to learn from the example of the early disciples.

1. Read 2 Timothy 1:8 and then answer the following questions.

    a. What did Paul, who was imprisoned in Rome, ask of Timothy?

    b. Is this what you would have expected him to ask? Why or why not?

    c. In what ways would knowing that Timothy was doing this have encouraged Paul? How would it encourage suffering believers today?

2. What kind of encouragement did John offer to Christians who were experiencing severe suffering persecution for Jesus? In what ways would this message encourage suffering believers today? (See Revelation 1:9.)

3. Few people have ever had the passion for walking as Jesus walked that Paul had, yet he longed for the support and care of the body of Christ when he suffered. Read Philippians 1:3–8 and 4:14–19 and notice the example that is set for us.

   a. How aware of and concerned for Paul's suffering were the Philippians?

   b. What did his relationship with the Philippian believers mean to Paul? Take note of the words Paul used that show the affection and the intimacy of their concern for one another.

   c. In what ways did the Philippians bless Paul? How did God view their actions?

4. Since the Roman authorities had apparently accused Paul of treason, what risks might a person have taken to support and encourage Paul during his imprisonment in Rome? (See 2 Timothy 1:15–18.)

   a. How had most of the believers responded to Paul while he was in Rome?

b. What had the "household" (usual term for *church*) of Onesiphorus done for Paul, and at what risk? How deeply did Paul appreciate it?

c. Put yourself in Paul's place, or in Rebecca's place if that is easier for you, and imagine what it would mean to you if a fellow believer sought you out and ministered to your needs in the midst of your suffering.

What Can You Do?

If you are not being persecuted, God still commands you to enter the experience of believers who are suffering and to suffer with them! One way to do this is to pray regularly for them. You can pray for:

- The deepening of our sense of community with believers in other places and cultures.
- Government leaders in your country, in other countries, and leaders of world organizations, that they will act and speak justly for the relief of suffering believers.
- Organizations that advocate for persecuted believers.
- The world to see the power of Jesus at work in the lives of innocent believers who courageously face martyrdom.
- Jesus to come quickly so that all suffering will end and he will be honored as Lord of Lords and King of Kings.

Reflection

Encouragement in the body of Christ doesn't just come from those who are spared suffering. Those in the body who are suffering have much to share with those who are not. From his confinement in Rome, Paul wrote as a suffering servant of God to the believers at Colosse. Read Colossians 2:1–3, 5.

How was Paul walking as Jesus walked? In what ways does his relationship with the Colossians show that he was being a disciple who makes disciples?

Does the suffering of other believers help you become a more faithful disciple? Does their faithfulness in the midst of suffering encourage you to walk with Jesus with greater passion and boldness? Why or why not? If so, why is it important for you to know about and be involved with the struggles of suffering believers?

What has your attitude been toward the suffering of Christians in other places of the world? What are the consequences when you, and other believers, forget about the suffering other members of Jesus' "body" are experiencing?

What are some practical ways in which you can become more informed about the persecution of believers and join with them in their suffering for Jesus? What specific things can you do to help alleviate the suffering of Christians in such places as India, China, Saudi Arabia, Sudan, Nigeria, and Iraq?

Pray

Ask God to give you the courage to face whatever comes as you seek to walk as Jesus walked. Ask him to make you more sensitive to the suffering of other believers—here and in other countries—and to be thankful for their sacrifices on your behalf. Pray that you will feel their pain more deeply and be more willing to live passionately for God, doing whatever you can to support suffering members of the body so they are not forgotten.

How You Can Learn More

The Voice of the Martyrs is an organization dedicated to informing the world (especially Jesus' followers) of the plight of persecuted Christians worldwide. To learn more about suffering believers, check out this website: *VoiceoftheMartyrs@www.persecution.com.*

Bibliography

Books

Akurgal, Ekrem. *Ancient Civilizations and Ruins of Turkey*. Istanbul: Haset Kitabevi, 1985.

Bayram, Tekin, ed. *First International Congress on Antioch of Pisidia: A Collection of Scholarly Papers*. Yalvac, Turkey: Kocaeli, 1997.

Beitzel, Barry J. *Moody Bible Atlas of Bible Lands*. Chicago: Moody Press, 1993.

Byfield, Ted, ed. *The Christians: Their First Two Thousand Years* (vol. 1: *The Veil Is Torn*, 2002; vol. 2: *A Pinch of Incense*, 2002; vol. 3: *By This Sign*, 2003). Canada: Friesens Corporation.

Cohen, Shaye J. D. "Was Timothy Jewish? (Acts 16:1 – 3)" *Journal of Biblical Literature*, 105/2, 1986.

Cole, Dan P. "Corinth and Ephesus: Why did Paul Spend Half His Journeys in These Cities?" *Bible Review*, December 1988.

DeVries, LaMoine F. *Cities of the Biblical World*. Peabody, Mass.: Hendrickson, 1997.

Dobson, James. *When God Doesn't Make Sense*. Wheaton, Ill.: Tyndale, 1993.

Edmonds, Anna G. *Turkey's Religious Sites*. Istanbul: Damko, 1997.

Fant, Clyde E., and Mitchell G. Reddish. *A Guide to Biblical Sites in Greece and Turkey*. London: Oxford University Press, 2003.

Feldman, Louis H. "Financing the Colosseum," *Biblical Archaeology Review*, July/August 2001.

Fitzmyer, Joseph A. *The Acts of the Apostles*, The Anchor Bible Commentary Series. New York: Doubleday, 1997.

Fox, Robin Lane. *Pagans and Christians*. New York: Penguin Books, 1988.

Foxe, John, and William Byron Forbush, ed. *Foxe's Book of Martyrs: A History of the Lives, Sufferings and Triumphant Deaths of the Early Christian and Protestant Martyrs*. Peabody, Mass.: Hendrickson Christian Classics, 2004.

Fredriksen, Paula. "Paul at the Races." *Bible Review*, June 2002.

Frend, W. H. C. *Martyrdom and Persecution in the Early Church*. London: Oxford University Press, 1965.

Gardiner, E. N. *Athletics of the Ancient World*. London: Oxford University Press, 1930.

Gill, David, and Conrad Gempf. *The Book of Acts in Its Greco-Roman Setting* (vol. 2 of 6-vol. series, The Book of Acts in Its First-Century Setting). Grand Rapids, Mich.: Eerdmans, 1994.

Gradel, Ittai. *Emperor Worship and Roman Religion*. London: Oxford University Press, 2004.

Gwatkin, W. *Cappadocia as a Roman Procuratorial Province*. Princeton, N.J.: Princeton University Press, 1930.

Hamilton, Edith. *Mythology*. New York: Penguin Books, 1969.

Harris, H. A. *Sport in Greece and Rome*. London: Thames and Hudson, 1972.

Hegg, Tim. *The Letter Writer: Paul's Background and Torah Perspective*. First Fruits of Zion, 2002.

Jeffers, James S. *The Greco-Roman World of the New Testament Era*. Downers Grove, Ill.: InterVarsity Press, 1999.

Jones, A. H. M. *The Cities of the Eastern Roman Provinces*, 2nd ed. London: Oxford University Press, 1971.

Kraybill, J. Nelson. *Imperial Cult and Commerce in John's Apocalypse*. Sheffield, Eng.: Academic Press, 1996.

Kushner, Harold S. *When Bad Things Happen to Good People*. New York: Random House, 1981.

Levick, B. M. *Roman Colonies in Southern Asia Minor*. London: Oxford University Press, 1967.

Levinskaya, Irina. *The Book of Acts in Its Diaspora Setting* (vol. 5 of 6-vol. series, The Book of Acts in Its First-Century Setting). Grand Rapids, Mich.: Eerdmans, 1994.

Meeks, W. A. *The First Urban Christians*. New Haven, Conn.: Yale University Press, 1982.

Murphy-O'Connor, Jerome. "Prisca and Aquila." *Bible Review*, December 1992.

Musurillo, H. *The Acts of the Christian Martyrs*. London: Oxford University Press, 1972.

Nanos, Mark D. *The Galatians Debate.* Peabody, Mass.: Hendrickson, 2002.

Olivova, Vera. *Sports and Games in the Ancient World.* London: Orbis, 1984.

Pixner, Bargil. *The Fifth Gospel: With Jesus Through Galilee.* Rosh Pina, Israel: Corazin Publishing, 1992.

Robertson, James. *Here I Am, God; Where Are You?* Wheaton, Ill.: Tyndale, 1976.

Safrai, Shmuel, M. Stern, D. Flusser, and W. C. Van Unnik. *The Jewish People in the First Century,* 9 vols. Amsterdam: Van Gorcum, 1974.

Saint Croix, G. E. M. "Aspects of the Great Persecution." *Harvard Theological Review,* 47:73–113, 1954.

Saint Croix, G. E. M. "Why Were the Early Christians Persecuted?" *Past and Present,* 26:1–38, 1964.

Saint Croix, G. E. M., and A. J. Toynbee, eds. *Christianity's Encounter with the Roman Imperial Government.* London: The Crucible of Christianity, 1969.

Sanders, E. P. *Paul and Palestinian Judaism.* Minneapolis: Fortress, 1977.

Scanlon, Thomas F. *Greek and Roman Athletics* Chicago: Ares, 1984.

Stauffer, Ethelbert. *Christ and the Caesars.* Philadelphia: Westminster Press, 1955.

Stendahl, Krister. *Paul Among Jews and Gentiles.* Philadelphia: Fortress, 1976.

Sullivan, R. D. *Near Eastern Royalty and Rome, 100–300 BC.* Toronto: University of Toronto Press, 1990.

Valavanis, Panos. *Games and Sanctuaries in Ancient Greece.* Los Angeles: Getty Publications, 2004.

Visalli, Gayla. *After Jesus: The Triumph of Christianity.* New York: Reader's Digest, 1992.

Ward, Kaari. *Jesus and His Times.* New York: Reader's Digest, 1987.

Winter, Bruce W., and Andrew D. Clarke. *Ancient Literary Setting* (vol. 1 of 6-vol. series, The Book of Acts in Its First-Century Setting). Grand Rapids, Mich.: Eerdmans, 1994.

Wright, N. T. "Paul, A Leader of a Jewish Revolution." *Bible Review,* December 2000.

Wright, N. T. "Paul's Challenge to Caesar." *Bible Review*, April 1999.

Wright, N. T. "Upstaging the Emperor." *Bible Review*, February 1998.

Wright, N. T. *What Saint Paul Really Said*. Grand Rapids, Mich.: Eerdmans, 1997.

Yamauchi, Edwin. *The Archaeology of New Testament Cities in Western Asia Minor*. Grand Rapids, Mich.: Baker, 1980.

Young, Brad H. *Paul the Jewish Theologian*. Peabody, Mass.: Hendrickson, 1997.

Websites

www.anistor.co.hol.gr/english/enback/CJLyes_Roman_Persecution_Xian.pdf, 2005, Anistoriton.

www.archaeoexpeditions.com/turkey.html, 2005, ArchaeoExpeditions—Turkey.

www.arthistory.sbc.edu/imageswomen/papers/lombardiaphrodite/aphrodite.html, 2005, Sweet Briar College.

www.atamanhotel.com/pisidia.html, 2005, Ataman Hotel & Restaurant.

www.biblicalturkeyguide.com/pisidian_antioch.htm, 2005, Biblical Turkey.

www.bridgesforpeace.com/publications/teaching/Article–34.html, 2005, Bridges for Peace: Your Israel Connection.

www.ccel.org/f/foxe/martyrs/, 2005, Christian Classics Ethereal Library.

www.cryingvoice.com/Christian_martyrs/TenPersIntro.html, 2005, Crying Voice in the Wilderness: Christian Martyrs.

www.csun.edu/~hcfll004/sportbib.html, 2005, Sport in Greek Antiquity: A Brief Bibliography.

www.ctsp.co.il/LBS%20pages/LBS_pisidian_antioch.htm, 2005, Christian Travel Study Programs.

www.ctsp.co.il/LBS%20pages/LBS_lystra.htm, 2005, Christian Travel Study Programs, Ltd.

www.ctsp.co.il/LBS%20pages/LBS_derbe.htm, 2005, Christian Travel Study Programs, Ltd.

www.depthome.brooklyn.cuny.edu/classics/gladiatr/index.htm, 2005, Roman Gladiatorial Games.

www.earlychurch.org.uk/persecution.html, 2005, EarlyChurch.org.uk: An Internet Resource for Studying the Early Church.

www.earlychurch.org.uk/persecution-russell.html, 2005, EarlyChurch.org. uk: An Internet Resource for Studying the Early Church.

www.ella.slis.indiana.edu/~zestrada/Antioch/, 2005, Antioch of Pisidia: The University of Michigan's 1924 Archaeological Expedition.

www.en-gedi.org/, 2005, En-Gedi Resource Center.

www.exploreturkey.com/exptur.phtml?id=39, 2005, Explore Turkey.

www.goturkey.turizm.gov.tr/destinasyon_en.asp?BELGENO=9661&baslik=Y alvac& belgekod=9661, 2005, Republic of Turkey Ministry of Culture and Tourism.

www.historyinfilm.com/claudius/classics/12caesar/julius2.htm, 2005, History in Film.

www.insaph.kcl.ac.uk/ala2004/index.html, 2005, Aphrodisias in Late Antiquity.

www.ku.edu/carrie/texts/carrie_books/seaver, 2005, The University of Kansas: Carrie Books — *Persecution of the Jews in the Roman Empire*, by James Everett Seaver.

www.kultur.gov.tr/portal/arkeoloji_en.asp?belgeno=669, 2005, Turkey Ministry of Culture and Tourism.

www.luthersem.edu/ckoester/Paul/Early/Main.htm, 2005, Luther Seminary.

www.netivyah.org.il/English%20Web/MidrashaArticles/paul_synagogue.html, 2005, Netivyah Bible Instruction Ministry.

www.newadvent.org/cathen/09478c.htm, 2005, New Advent.

www.nyu.edu/projects/aphrodisias/home.ti.htm, 2005, New York University.

www.philipharland.com/articleSR.htm, 2005, The Web Site of Philip A. Harland.

www.request.org.uk/main/history/romans/romans03.htm, 2005, Re:Quest (a free website for teaching about Christianity in Religious Education).

www.sailturkey.com/panoramas/aphrodisias, 2005, sailturkey.com.

www.turizm.net/cities/aphrodisias/, 2005, Turizm.net.

www.turizm.net/cities/yalvac/index.html, 2005, Turizm.net.

www.turkeytours.com/Cappadocia.html, 2005, turkeytours.com.

www.unbound.biola.edu/acts/index.cfm?lang=English&item=pantiochl, 2005, The Unbound Bible — Biola University.

www.unbound.biola.edu/acts/index.cfm?lang=English&item=derbel, 2005, The Unbound Bible — Biola University.

www.unbound.biola.edu/acts/index.cfm?lang=English&item=lystral, 2005, The Unbound Bible — Biola University.

www.users.drew.edu/ddoughty/Christianorigins/persecutions/bibper99.html,
   2005, Drew University: BIBST 702S: Persecution and Martyrdom in
   Early Christianity.

www.wildwinds.com/coins/greece/pisidia/antioch/t.html, 2005, Wildwinds
   (online reference, attribution & valuation site for ancient Greek,
   Roman & Byzantine coins).

www.worldinvisible.com/library/sauer/5f00.0747/5f00.0747.3.htm, 2005, World
   Invisible.

We want to hear from you. Please send your comments about this book to us in care of zreview@zondervan.com. Thank you.

ZONDERVAN.com/
AUTHORTRACKER
follow your favorite authors